A GUIDE TO THE
National Curriculum

SECOND EDITION

Bob Moon

OXFORD UNIVERSITY PRESS

Oxford University Press, Walton Street, Oxford OX2 6DP

Oxford New York Toronto
Delhi Bombay Calcutta Madras Karachi
Kuala Lumpur Singapore Hong Kong Tokyo
Nairobi Dar es Salaam Cape Town
Melbourne Auckland Madrid

and associated companies in
Berlin Ibadan

Oxford is a trade mark of Oxford University Press

First published 1991
Second edition 1994

British Library Cataloguing in Publication Data
Data available

Library of Congress Cataloging in Publication Data
Data available
ISBN 0-19-288000-4

10 9 8 7 6 5 4 3 2

Printed in Great Britain
by Biddles Ltd.
Guildford & King's Lynn

A Guide to the National Curriculum

...reviews of the first edition:

'clear, comprehensive . . . essential for the staffroom shelf'

Juliet Hobson, *Times Educational Supplement*

'useful . . . Parents and governors should certainly find it informative . . . up-to-date [and] readable'

Michael Salter, *Education*

Preface

A wide range of people have contributed to the information and ideas within this guide. For the first edition, officers from the National Councils provided advice on points of detail, and the likely direction of policy in the future. Keith Hedger and Michael Raleigh of Shropshire provided a useful detailed commentary on the guide. My colleagues Janet Maybin, Patricia Murphy, Christine Shiu, and Will Swann looked at specific sections. For the second edition, more detailed commentary on each of the subjects within the National Curriculum has been provided. Academic staff working on the new Open University Postgraduate Certificate in Education have revised and developed the original entries. These include for each core subject: Sue Brindley on English, Michelle Selinger on mathematics, and Ralph Levinson on science. For the OU foundation subjects: Hilary Bourdillon on history, Frank Banks on technology, and Ann Swarbrick on modern languages. Jill Bourne has revised the entries relating to primary schooling and Ann Shelton Mayes the section on assessment. Elizabeth Freeman and Julie Herbert have provided the necessary administrative and secretarial support. Finally I would like to thank Barbara Vander, who first suggested that a guide such as this would be of interest and value to those coming new to the National Curriculum.

B.M.

Oxford
August 1993

Contents

Introduction

The National Curriculum, introduced in 1988 as part of the Education Reform Act, represents one of the most significant educational reforms this century. It is a public statement about the syllabus and content that every child should study until he or she leaves school. It is important for teachers and parents to understand the structure and terminology of the curriculum as a whole and the individual subjects within it. This is particularly so for teachers in training and for the thousands of parents playing an active role on governing bodies and parent–teacher associations.

This guide:

- provides an introduction to the way the National Curriculum is organized in primary, secondary, and middle schools;
- explains the meanings of the terms used on a daily basis now by teachers and by pupils;
- outlines the content of the different subjects;
- gives guidance on the systems of assessment and testing used;
- sets out the entitlement parents have in relation to their child's progress;
- explores a number of the controversial issues associated with the early years of National Curriculum development in schools.

In using this guide, two important points need to be borne in mind. First it does not attempt to serve as a substitute for the statutory orders, official regulations, and formal documentation associated with the National Curriculum. Some of the documentation is daunting, even for the interested reader, but it does prescribe the legal basis upon which the National Curriculum is based. Regular changes have occurred in the content of some of the subjects, and the way testing and assessment is organized, and it is necessary to refer to the official publications for the precise legal situation at any one time or in respect of a particular age group. These publications are quite expensive, but all schools keep copies and can make them available to parents. It is especially important to note that in Wales and in Northern Ireland there are differences from the prescribed arrangements in England. Examples in the text illustrate these differences (particular attention is given to this in the entry on history, where the differences are most marked), and they are set out in full in official documents produced by the National Councils in both Cardiff and Belfast (see Further Reading). This leads to a second point. The information and guidance set out in this guide are both supplemented by contact and involvement with schools. Early experience with the National Curriculum has shown that schools require greater flexibility than was envisaged in 1988, and changes have been introduced to permit this. A review of the national curriculum carried out by Sir Ron Dearing, Chairman of the Schools Curriculum and Assessment Authority (SCAA) will lead to changes to the legal requirements in each of the subjects. These, however, will not be implemented in schools before September 1995. It is very important therefore to look at how a national framework described in this guide is developed at the school level. A central core of curriculum opportunities and entitlement for all children is, however, now enshrined in law, with political support across all major parties, and the National Curriculum will be one of the cornerstones of school development in the 1990s and through to the twenty-first century. This guide is a contribution to ensuring that it is appreciated and understood by everyone with an interest and involvement in education.

1 What is the National Curriculum?

In order to understand the National Curriculum, you will first need to become familiar with a small number of terms and phrases. These are straightforward not only for teachers, governors, and parents but also, perhaps with the exception of the very youngest, for pupils in schools.

The National Curriculum forms an important part of the Education Reform Act that became law in the summer of 1988. The aims of the new curriculum, set out in Clause 2, are to prescribe a number of school subjects and specify in relation to each:

- the knowledge, skills, and understanding which pupils of different abilities and maturities are expected to have;
- the matters, skills, and processes which are required to be taught to pupils of different abilities and maturities;
- arrangements for assessing pupils.

Core and other foundation subjects

The National Curriculum is described as ten subjects. Three of the subjects are defined as *core foundation* subjects and seven merely as *foundation* subjects. Most of the subjects are well known and have featured in school curricula for many years.

Core foundation subjects[1]	English, mathematics, science
Foundation subjects	Art, geography, history, modern language, music, physical education, technology

The original plan was to teach all ten subjects through to the age of 16, with the exception of modern languages, which would only be

---

[1] In Wales, Welsh is also taught as a core foundation subject where the medium of instruction in the school is Welsh. In all other Welsh schools, it is one of the foundation subjects.

introduced at the secondary II+ age group. This has now been modified, and from the age of 14 many of the subjects have become optional. The core foundation subjects, however, remain compulsory through to the end of year II, the end of compulsory schooling.

Schools are also required, as they always have been, to teach religious education. However, this is not one of the ten subjects of the National Curriculum, and arrangements for drawing up an agreed syllabus are made at the local education authority, not national, level.

In the way the National Curriculum has developed there is little legal distinction between the core foundation and foundation subjects. The Secretary of State was required to introduce the three core subjects before any others, but the way the content is described is the same for each of the ten subjects. Four terms are used to describe each subject:

- programmes of study;
- attainment targets and strands;
- levels of attainment;
- statements of attainment.

Programmes of study

The ways in which the attainment targets and statements of attainment are to be taught are set out in *programmes of study* (PoS). Teachers and schools are bound to follow these; they give more information to teachers about contents, methods, and approaches. An example of a programme of study for mathematics reads as follows:

Pupils should engage in activities which involve recognising that multiplication and division are inverse operations, and using this to check calculations. (Maths 2, Algebra, level 4)

Attainment targets and strands

Each subject is defined by *attainment targets* (AT) that all pupils must have the opportunity to study. In mathematics, for example, there are five such targets, each broken down into strands that provide an indication of the sort of syllabus the attainment target will cover:

AT1.	Using and Applying Mathematics	(i)	Applications
		(ii)	Mathematical communication
		(iii)	Reasoning, logic, and proof
AT2.	Number	(i)	Knowledge and use of numbers
		(ii)	Estimation and approximation
		(iii)	Measures
AT3.	Algebra	(i)	Patterns and relationships
		(ii)	Formulae, equations, and inequalities
		(iii)	Graphical representation
AT4.	Shape and Space	(i)	Shape
		(ii)	Location
		(iii)	Movement
		(iv)	Measures
AT5.	Handling Data	(i)	Collecting and processing
		(ii)	Representing and interpreting
		(iii)	Probability

Each attainment target is currently subdivided into ten levels of attainment. Level 1 corresponds to what might be achieved in the first year or so of schooling, and level 10 to the upper secondary years. In mathematics attainment target 2, Number, the infant would be expected to 'add and subtract using a small number of objects', whilst the most advanced secondary school pupils would be 'able to determine the possible effects of error in calculations'.

The ten levels at present also provide the basis for testing and assessing, and so it is common for a child's progress to be recorded in terms of a 1–10 score. In the first few years of the National Curriculum the reliability and validity of this system were questioned, and it is now planned that the scale will not apply to pupils in the 14–16 age range.

The levels as they are set out in the National Curriculum are depicted by *statements of attainment*. These give a brief indication of the sort of work children should be doing at that level. The attainment targets and the statements of attainment are central to the National Curriculum. The former act like the trunk of a tree, with the latter forming the branches. In attainment target 4, Shape and Space, in mathematics, this is set out in the following way (pp. 6–9):

Programme of study	Statements of attainment	Examples
Level 2		
• Recognizing squares, rectangles, circles, triangles, hexagons, pentagons, cubes, rectangular boxes (cuboids), cylinders, and spheres and describing their properties.	(a) Use mathematical terms to describe common 2D shapes and 3D objects.	Create pictures and patterns using 2D shapes and describe them. Describe 3D objects using appropriate language.
• Recognizing right-angled corners in 2D and 3D shapes.		
• Recognizing types of movement: straight (translation), turning (rotation).	(b) Recognize different types of movement.	Rotate body through 1, 2, 3, and 4 right angles. Turn to left or right on instructions (in PE, games using turtle graphics, or programmable toys).
• Understanding angle as a measurement of turn.		
• Understanding turning through right angles.		
• Understanding the conservation of length, capacity, and 'weight'.		
Level 3		
• Sorting 2D and 3D shapes and giving reasons for each method of sorting.	(a) Sort shapes using mathematical criteria and give reasons.	Sort shapes with a square corner, shapes with curved edges, and shapes with equal sides or faces, giving appropriate explanations.

Programme of study	Statements of attainment	Examples
• Recognizing (reflective) symmetry in a variety of shapes in two and three dimensions.	(b) Recognize reflective symmetry.	Explore patterns from a variety of world cultures, e.g. Islamic, Japanese. Study shapes and identify some lines and planes of symmetry. Explore patterns in art or PE.
• Using and understanding compass bearings and the terms 'clockwise' and 'anticlockwise'	(c) Use the eight points of the compass to show direction.	Describe wind direction from a weather-vane. Describe locations of places in the neighbourhood of the school, using compass points.
Level 4		
• Constructing simple 2D and 3D shapes from given information knowing associated language.	(a) Construct 2D or 3D shapes and know associated language.	Construct rectangles, circles, nets for cubes, pyramids, and prisms.
• Reflecting simple shapes in a mirror line.		Know 'acute', 'obtuse', 'reflex', 'parallel', 'perpendicular', 'vertical', 'horizontal', etc.
• Understanding the congruence of simple shapes.		Design and make a container for an awkwardly shaped object, e.g. 'Santa's lost boot'.
• Understanding and using language associated with angle.		

Programme of study	Statements of attainment	Examples
• Specifying location by means of coordinates in the first quadrant and by means of angle and distance.	(b) Specify location.	Locate features on an ordnance survey map given their grid references. Use turtle graphics instructions for distances and direction.
• Recognizing rotational symmetry.	(c) Recognize rotational symmetry.	Confirm the rotational symmetry of shapes using tracing paper.
• Finding perimeters of simple shapes.	(d) Find perimeters, areas, or volumes.	Identify different rectangles with the same perimeter. Compare the areas of leaves using a transparent square grid. Work out the approximate volumes of small boxes. Work out how many different rectangles can be made from twenty-four tiles. What is their area and perimeter?
• Finding areas by counting squares, and volumes by counting cubes.		

Level 5

• Measuring and drawing angles to the nearest degree.	(a) Use accurate measurement and drawing in constructing 3D models	Construct prisms. Make a pyramid-shaped gift box of given dimensions.

Programme of study	Statements of attainment	Examples
• Explaining and using properties associated with intersecting and parallel lines and triangles, and knowing associated language.	(b) Use properties of shape to justify explanations.	Give reasons when identifying equal angles in a diagram. Find the centres, axes, and planes of symmetry in a variety of plane and solid shapes.
• Identifying the symmetries of various shapes.		
• Using networks to solve problems.	(c) Use networks to solve problems.	Find the shortest route for a person delivering the post.
• Specifying location by means of coordinates in four quadrants.		
• Finding areas of plane figures (excluding circles), using appropriate formulae.	(d) Find areas of plane shapes or volumes of simple solids.	Know and use the formulae for finding the areas of squares, rectangles, triangles.
• Finding volumes of simple solids (excluding cylinders), using appropriate formulae.		Find the volumes of cubes, cuboids, and triangular prisms.
• Finding the circumference of circles, practically, introducing the ratio p.		

The number of statements of attainment varies at each level. In the example above there are three at level 3, and four at level 5. Over the last few years there has been considerable criticism that the National Curriculum had been set down in too much detail. It is likely therefore that more simplified versions than currently exist will be developed.

It is important to remember that in the classroom statements of attainment and even attainment targets are not dealt with one at a time. Many themes and issues set out in the programme of study allow more than one attainment target and certainly more than one statement of attainment to be covered at the same time. Teaching in the National Curriculum could be compared with learning to ride a bicycle, drive a car, or develop expertise with computers. As you learn, you have to develop a variety of skills. Every so often you may concentrate on just one, but always in the context of the others. You may (as at the end of a driving test) at moments of assessment need to separate the different techniques and areas of knowledge, to ensure that progress can be measured and the areas for improvement identified.

So far, we have met three key terms which are used in National Curriculum statutory orders. The attainment targets and statements of attainment provide a structured shorthand that illustrates the scope of work required of pupils. Assessments, either by teachers or through externally set tasks, will be made against these. Programmes of study are equally important for teachers implementing the National Curriculum, and you should refer to the published statutory orders (see Further Reading) if you want to see them in full.

Key stages

The law states what should be taught in stages, rather than in school years. The years 5–16 have been classified into four *key stages* (KS), each covering two or three years of schooling:

key stage 1: 5–7-year-olds;
key stage 2: 9–11-year-olds;
key stage 3: 11–14-year-olds;
key stage 4: 14–16-year-olds.

To simplify a child's progress, each of the years of schooling has been given a number from year 1 (the first year) to year 11 (the final year of compulsory secondary schooling). This will sound unfamiliar to most adults, who will perhaps remember being in the first year at secondary school and progressing on to the fifth year to take examinations. There were, however, many confusions around, particularly when the age of transfer for pupils in secondary schooling varied from the normal II+ and in those parts of the country where middle schools existed. Most schools now use the numbering system described below:

Key stage	New description	Age of majority of pupils at the end of the school year
	Rª	5
1	Y1	6
	Y2	7
2	Y3	8
	Y4	9
	Y5	10
	Y6	11
3	Y7	12
	Y8	13
	Y9	14
4	Y10	15
	Y11	16
	Y12ª	17
	Y13ª	18

Note: R = Reception; Y = Year.

ª Reception and Y12–Y13 are not covered by National Curriculum legislation.

Using key stages as a structure, rather than ages or years, is a characteristic of the National Curriculum. For each subject, the range of levels that most children up to the age of fourteen will work through is described. Examples for the core foundation subjects and technology are set out in tables such as that on the next page.

Subject	KS1 (5–7 years)	KS2 (7–11 years)	KS3 (11–14 years)
Mathematics	1–3	2–6	3–8
Science	1–3	2–5	3–7
English	1–3	2–5	3–8
Welsh	1–3	2–5	3–8
Welsh second language	1–3	2–5	3–8/1–6[a]
Technology	1–3	2–5	3–7
Modern foreign languages	—	—	1–10
History	1–3	2–5	3–7
Geography	1–3	2–5	3–7

[a] For those beginning Welsh second language at 11.

In developing the National Curriculum it was decided that there would not be an attempt to link levels of attainment in art, music, and physical education to the key stages. The level of detail was inappropriate and it was not expected that there would be the same degree of extended testing and assessment as in the other subjects.

The chart is only a guideline, based on what pupils of different ages achieve now in school. Many individual children will achieve higher levels than these average figures suggest. Over the coming years standards may change.

The programmes of study, attainment targets, and statements of attainment around which teaching and learning are planned were initially established by working parties appointed by the Secretary of State. These produced reports which were the basis for consultation, and, under the Education Reform Act, the form taken by the final statutory orders laid before Parliament is a ministerial decision. There is an overall plan showing when the different subjects become part of the National Curriculum, and when they become a statutory requirement at the different key stages (see Chapter 9).

The Education Reform Act does not lay down for how long or for what percentage of the week each subject should be studied. Subsequent regulations only talk of providing a reasonable amount of time, which permits schools to organize their schemes of work to allow for worthwhile study by each pupil of the 'knowledge, skills and understanding, including processes, normally associated with the foundation subjects' (from a Department of Education and Science publication *National Curriculum: From Policy to Practice* distributed free to all teachers when the reforms were introduced).

There has been much speculation about how time is best divided up, especially at the upper secondary level, where the timetable usually allows a certain percentage of time (about 10 per cent) for each subject and half that for short courses. Responsibility for these decisions lies with the school and in particular with the governing board. It is wise to check the curriculum arrangements for key stage 4 with the school or the local education authority.

It is important to remember that schools do not have to teach in subjects. Very few, if any, primary schools divide the school week up into ten or eleven subjects, and many secondary schools combine certain subject areas for teaching purposes. History and geography, for example, may become humanities; music and art may be part of the overall arts provision that includes dance and drama. This poses no difficulties, and may have certain advantages as long as attention is given to the content of the National Curriculum subject areas, and provided, where programmes of study, attainment targets, and statements of attainment are laid down in statutory orders, that the requirements are met. There are many ways in which schools can set out to do this. The particular style and approach chosen has to be agreed by the school governors, who in turn report to parents. Information about the curriculum must also be given in the school prospectus. Chapter 8 explains these requirements in some detail.

Whatever the structure of the curriculum, there is a further dimension to the National Curriculum that both primary and secondary schools will have to incorporate in their plans.

Whole-curriculum dimensions, skills, and themes

A well-balanced curriculum represents more than the sum total of the subjects within it. The more integrated planning of most primary schools has already been mentioned; but in both primary and secondary schools teachers now develop plans that show how important issues are carried across as well as within subjects. These are not legally binding, although the Schools Curriculum and Assessment Authority (SCAA), the body responsible for overseeing the National Curriculum in England, provides advice and guidance as to how this is done. Three aspects of whole-curriculum planning have been identified:

- *Dimensions*: these refer to aspects such as ensuring equal opportunities for all pupils in the curriculum and educating pupils for life in a multicultural society.
- *Skills*: various skills needed by pupils appear in many subjects: communication, numeracy, study skills, problem-solving, personal and social skills, and information technology are the six identified by SCAA.
- *Themes*: there are important aspects of the curriculum which sometimes appear as a subject in themselves but can also be developed across the curriculum and subjects as a whole; these include economic and industrial understanding, career education and guidance, health education, citizenship, and environmental education.

A final point

It must be emphasized that the National Curriculum does not cover the whole of the school curriculum. Indeed, in the period since 1988 there have been significant moves to ensure that the legal part of the curriculum does not take up the whole of the time allocated. Children will study subjects and take part in activities that are additional to those set out in the statutory orders. In Key Stage 1–3 some 20% of curriculum time has been freed to be used at the school's discretion. In Key Stage 4 the minimum requirements have been reduced to English, mathematics, a single science, plus short courses in a modern foreign language, technology, and physical education. This requirement, along with RE, leaves a considerable amount of time for a diverse range of courses planned by the school. School prospectuses, and the curriculum information that must now be provided to parents, will show how the National Curriculum requirements fit into the particular plans developed within individual schools.

2   Why a National Curriculum?

Advocates of a National Curriculum can be found right across the political spectrum. It is highly unlikely that changes in government would lead to the total repeal of the legislation, and it is now clear that a National Curriculum will be part of the educational scene for the foreseeable future.

Differences between schools

For many educationists the logic that underpins the provision of free and compulsory schooling also extends to what is taught. In arguing for a National Curriculum, they point to glaring inconsistencies between schools. In the same locality, one primary school may have had a fully worked-out science scheme, and another school no science scheme at all. Even if both schools did have plans for teaching science, there would be no guarantee that they would approach the subject in similar ways. One school might have attempted to achieve a balance between the different scientific disciplines (physics, chemistry, biology, and perhaps astronomy and earth sciences). The other, however, could have leaned heavily on the tradition of nature study—the sort of primary science that most parents remember from their own school-days. In other subjects similar differences existed. A survey by Her Majesty's Inspectorate at the end of the 1980s showed how haphazard the teaching of history and geography could be. It pointed to the lack of any attempt in many schools to ensure that children came into contact with progressively more demanding ideas, skills, and concepts.

Inequality of provision

In secondary schools the existence of different curriculum opportunities could be seen clearly. Girls, for example, often chose to drop the physical sciences in favour of biology. Boys significantly outnumbered girls in the technology classes that became increasingly available in the decade prior to the passing of the 1988 Education Reform Act. In a similar way, boys had very little contact with home economics. The number of students opting to study modern languages through to the end of year 11 or 13 was considerably less than in other subjects, and overall standards naturally appeared lower than in many other European countries. A National Curriculum provides a framework that could rule out such inconsistencies and inequalities.

Raising standards

Many supporters of the National Curriculum were also motivated by the desire to improve the quality of schooling and raise standards. The debate over standards has attracted media interest and controversy for many years. Some people have perceived a fall in standards of attainment in subjects such as English and mathematics. This is vigorously refuted by others, who point to the regular improvements in examination performance of both 16- and 18-year-olds, particularly in the 1960s and 1980s. For example, in 1970–1 16.6 per cent of the age group left school with one or more GCE A levels. By 1984–5 that percentage had increased to 18.1 per cent. In the same period the number of young people leaving school without A levels but with five or more higher grades in GCE/CSE or equivalent rose from 7.1 per cent to 10.3 per cent. Those with between one and four higher grades at GCE/CSE or equivalent rose from 16.9 per cent to 26.8 per cent, and those with one or more graded results rose from 9.8 per cent to 32.5 per cent. Those with no graded results fell from 44 per cent to 11.7 per cent. These comparisons have been taken from official DES statistics. Each year the publication of GCSE and A level results receives national attention and, overall, in each year there has been a gradual improvement in standards. About half of all the GCSE subjects taken are now graded at the higher level A–C, and the government has been inundated with candidates who, at A level, have the entry qualifications for university.

There are also reports from the Assessment of Performance Unit, set up in 1978 to monitor the extent to which standards vary over time. The work done by the unit shows how difficult a task this is. Knowledge is always evolving, and therefore the sort of tasks and questions that are appropriate in one decade may be redundant in the next. Extending the comparisons over more than a decade gives even greater difficulties. Changes in language usage make comparisons in English difficult. In mathematics the pound, shillings, and pence sums familiar to many parents could hardly be set today.

Despite the complexity and inconclusiveness of the debate, a political and media message about declining standards achieved widespread public acceptance. More than one Prime Minister has chosen to exploit the issue for political advantage. James Callaghan, in a famous speech at Ruskin College, Oxford, in 1976, talked of his concern at finding 'complaints from industry that new recruits from the schools sometimes do not have the basic tools to do the job that is required'. Margaret Thatcher in her 1987 speech to the Conservative Party Conference made a direct link between schooling and economic success: 'To compete successfully in tomorrow's world—against Japan, Germany and the United States—we need well-educated, well-trained, creative young people. If education is backward today, the national performance will be backward tomorrow.'

International comparisons represent a further dimension of the standards debate. Yet again, there are difficulties in coming to conclusive judgements. Setting tests that are comparable across a range of different countries and cultures has proved highly controversial. Assessments of practical and investigative work in science, for example, increasingly a feature of British science education, would be inappropriate in a different educational system where most teaching was through books and academic exercises. Some comparisons have been made that show how in mathematics and some aspects of science, British pupils do not attain such high standards as their Japanese equivalents. A 1988 publication by the International Associates for the Evaluation of Educational Achievement, *Science Achievement in Seventeen Countries*, showed that this was particularly true in the initial stages of secondary education, where England is listed with Hong Kong, Italy, Singapore, and the USA. These are all countries which the report says should be concerned about 'the scientific literacy of their general workforce'. Finland, Hungary, Japan, and Sweden led the field in mass secondary science attainment. The same report, however, shows that at more advanced levels Hong Kong, England, and Singapore together with Hungary and Japan would appear to be educating their élite relatively well.

Other research (see Figs. 1 and 2) shows British performance in mathematics to be around the mean of a range of countries where testing took place. The Centre for the Assessment of Educational Progress in the USA looked at average mathematics proficiency for 13-year-olds, and came to the conclusion that the South Koreans were the highest achievers, with the USA at the bottom of the league.

The question to ask is not whether standards are rising or falling, but whether we are satisfied with the 'mean score' of such international comparisons. These tests, however, only look at narrow and therefore comparable parts of mathematics and science. It would be very difficult to extend them to subjects such as drama or personal and social education. And we cannot be sure if high attainment in science or maths is achieved at the expense of other areas of school learning or experience that we value highly. Methods of teaching mathematics and science in Korea or Japan do not appear to place the same emphasis on developing problem-solving skills as in this country.

As we can see, the question of standards is a complex one. Are we

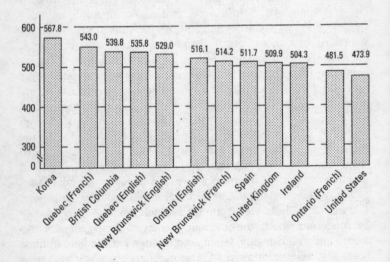

Fig.1   Average Mathematics Proficiency, Age 13.

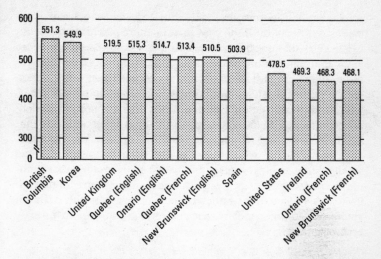

Fig.2 Average Science Proficiency, Age 13.

talking about achievements in specified subjects at certain ages? Are we thinking about the standards required to do a certain job, or to go on to further schooling or a profession? Are we merely comparing British pupils' performance at certain ages with similar groups in other industrialized countries? The list could go on. Are there, for example, differences between the north of the country and the south-east? How significant are urban and rural comparisons? The most important point to bear in mind when thinking of a National Curriculum is the potential of many young people, not necessarily the academic high-fliers, to become more confident and competent across a range of basic subjects. In the past, the expectations of what many children could achieve have been unnecessarily low. A defined framework, with attainment targets, could lead to higher expectations and improved standards; but how far this will be achieved will take many years to establish.

Improving communication

Creating a curriculum entitlement and raising standards are the two major justifications for a prescribed National Curriculum. There are, however, further supporting arguments. Many parents have found the curriculum a rather obscure part of the school's activities. There is some research evidence and a good deal of common-sense support for the view that the more parents know about what their children are expected to learn and achieve, the more likely the children are to succeed. Information such as this has been difficult for parents to obtain, not because of any obstruction on the part of teachers, but because there was no common language or agreed structure within which to explain or report on children's progress. Even where examination syllabuses existed, for GCSE or A level for example, parents could find it difficult to ascertain even roughly what point in the syllabus their child had reached. In many instances pupils would sit the examination without ever having seen the syllabus. The National Curriculum, with its relatively straightforward terminology, provides the basis for greater clarity in school–parent communication at both primary and secondary level.

Progress and continuity

The National Curriculum is an important means of improving the links between primary and secondary schools. Despite the existence of many well-organized liaison schemes, there has been much concern about the problems of transfer from primary to secondary schools. Secondary teachers receiving pupils from different primary schools have found it difficult to establish the subject content previously covered, or the level of attainment reached by individual children. It has not been unusual for secondary teachers to talk about 'starting from scratch'. This was particularly problematic in subjects where knowledge tends to build up sequentially, for example in mathematics, science, and perhaps music. A research study from the University of Leicester showed children actually falling back in attainment when moving schools. The National Curriculum provides a focus for better record-keeping and monitoring of progress between teachers and between schools.

All these arguments apply equally where forms of schooling other than primary and secondary exist. In some areas the existence of middle schools, or junior high schools, means that children have two changes of school, rather than the more usual one. Many families have to move from place to place because of job opportunities. Even within the same school, teachers move to new posts, fall ill, or are involved in in-service training. These events can lead to significant breaks in the continuity of children's education. Again, the National Curriculum is a means of minimizing disruption.

Individual attainment

Finally, there is one major potential advantage of the National Curriculum that could radically change the way school-days are experienced. Many parents will remember the monthly or termly 'position in class' lists compiled by form teachers. Similar lists were drawn up to describe the end-of-term examination results. Grading schemes might also have been used; in many schools A–E for attainment and 1–5 for effort were widely adopted in the 1970s and 1980s. Most of these schemes involved ranking pupils one against another, and in fact, throughout the twentieth century this has been the major form of assessment in British schools. Inevitably, a large proportion of pupils must come out as below average.

Rank order is most significant when it determines access to limited places, for example at universities or the administrative grades of the Civil Service. The public examination system served this purpose for most of this century. The 11+ examination, which selected about 20 per cent of the age group to go on to a grammar school education, is one of the best-known examples of rank ordering. The statistical model upon which the tests and examinations were based was the bell curve, with the bulk of the population (average performance) found at the top of the curve, and the most or least able on the extremities (see Fig. 3).

Many of those who have advocated a National Curriculum argue that we should be moving away from standards based on relative information (how one pupil compares with others) to absolute standards (whether a pupil has shown individual knowledge and competency in the different parts of the curriculum). Everyone should be able to achieve the higher levels of attainment, it is argued. The government-appointed Task Group on Assessment and Performance, set up to work out how the National Curriculum should be confined to 'the assessment of "performance" or "attainment," were not recommending any attempt to assess separately the problematic notion of underlying "ability"'.

This represents something of a challenge to school organizations where ranking still lives on. For the most part the 'position in class'

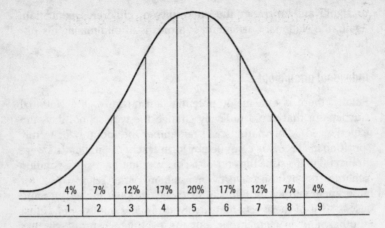

	4%	7%	12%	17%	20%	17%	12%	7%	4%
	1	2	3	4	5	6	7	8	9

Fig.3 Bell curve chart

lists have disappeared, but in teachers' and parents' minds the old idea, discredited by many of the developments in psychology, that children are born with a fixed potential, remains. The National Curriculum provides a national yardstick against which unrecognized potential can be realized and acknowledged.

3   The National Curriculum in the Classroom

Much of the work done in classrooms today will reflect the way teaching has evolved over many years. The look of the primary classroom as parents wait to collect their children at the end of the school day is very much the same as in pre-National Curriculum days, with children putting away books and pens, clearing up art materials, or perhaps tidying the reading-corner. The teacher might be asking two children to tell the rest of the class tomorrow morning about the plants they are growing in the school garden. In secondary schools, pupils will almost certainly have spent the day moving from one specialist area to another. Homework will have been set in certain of the core and foundation subjects. Some classes may have been asked to interview their parents about 'school-day memories' as part of a project in English. In many schools such a project will involve links with the history department. Sometimes there will have been class-centred lessons, with a teacher introducing a part of the scheme of work or syllabus and the pupils following this up with individual exercises or note-taking. In other classes, design tasks in technology, experiments in science, or a problem-solving exercise in mathematics may have involved pupils working together in groups of three or four.

The changes brought in by the National Curriculum which do affect teaching and classrooms can be summarized as follows:

- The way the curriculum is described is similar in primary and secondary schools. Programmes of study, attainment targets, and levels of attainment follow, as we have seen, right through the compulsory years of schooling.
- Each school and therefore each teacher now has the basis for a scheme of work which shows how the curriculum meets the

requirements of the National Curriculum. These are public documents that parents have the right to examine (see Chapter 8).

- There will be more recording of the work done in the classroom. Teachers will be looking to record which attainment targets have been covered and the level at which individual children are working. These records will form the basis for discussions with parents about the progress achieved.

- In many, perhaps all, schools the children will be encouraged to record their own progress through the schemes of work. Parents, for example, in talking to their children should be able to keep closely in touch with progress in between the regular meetings with class or subject teachers.

- In primary and secondary schools new programmes of technology have been introduced. Of all the National Curriculum subjects this has been the most difficult to develop. There is little surprise in this, since of all the ten subjects it is the one which has the most recent history of development. In many senses the first technology orders represented a new definition of the subject, and there have been teething problems. You will need to check to see how the ongoing reviews are affecting teaching at each of the key stages.

- At the secondary level all pupils will now study a modern language, probably through to the age of 16.

- In all schools teachers will have made plans to cover topics such as health education or career guidance through the schemes of work. Schools are not required by law to implement these cross-curricular themes, but are strongly encouraged to do so in guidance and advice.

In the next two sections examples show the National Curriculum at work in the classroom.

Planning the curriculum in the primary school

One major outcome of the introduction of the National Curriculum in the primary school has been an increase in whole school curriculum planning. The need to teach the content of the nine foundation subjects and RE to the level of detail required in the initial statutory orders would place a very heavy burden on the class teacher if left to a lone teacher and squeezed into the weekly timetable, especially at key stage 2. Most schools set up working groups led by the different subject curriculum leaders to analyse the requirements of the different subject orders at the different levels, and to draw up outline curriculum plans for key stage 1 and key stage 2. In this way the staff were able to pick out areas of 'overlap' between different subject areas, making the content rather more manageable. The table below, adapted from *A Framework for the Primary Curriculum*, a booklet of curriculum guidance produced by the National Curriculum Council, shows how the statements of attainment at level 2 for science, mathematics, and English overlap:

Science	English	Mathematics
Ask questions and suggest ideas of the 'how' and 'why' and 'what will happen if' variety.	Respond appropriately to a range of more complex instructions given by a teacher and give simple instructions.	Ask and respond to the question, 'What would happen if . . . ?'
Record findings in charts, drawings, and other appropriate forms.	Produce simple, coherent non-chronological writing.	Describe current work, record findings, and check results.
Be able to keep a diary, in a variety of forms, of change over time.	Structure sequences of real or imagined events coherently in chronological accounts.	Help to design a data-collection sheet and use it to record a set of data leading to a frequency table.

At the same time, schools were being encouraged to reappraise the common practice of primary planning in terms of integrated topics (sometimes called 'themes' or 'projects' or 'centres of interest'). Some examples of the sort of primary topics that were common are 'Ourselves', 'Transport', 'Flight', 'Homes'. Other teachers chose more general concepts as a central focus, such as 'Growth and Change' or 'Movement'.

The strength of planning within topics is that the learning that is offered to children is not fragmented into different subjects and presented in different slots in the children's day. A well-planned integrated curriculum allows children to follow an area up in depth, drawing on their own experience, and to explore the links between the different subjects. However, not all integrated curriculum planning was successful. There was some concern noted by HMI, in the 1992 DES report on the primary curriculum, for example, that topic work was sometimes undemanding, lacking in progression, and at worst amounted to little more than copying from books.

Whole school curriculum planning, then, had to analyse the National Curriculum requirements for each subject and to use these to redesign the curriculum to give breadth, balance, and continuity across the key stages, addressing criticisms such as those above. Topics began to be planned over a two-year cycle, with a different topic for each half-term. Each topic now tended to have a particular subject bias, so that teachers could ensure children worked on each of the foundation subject areas over a two-year cycle. An example over two terms from one school quoted in *Eating the Elephant Bit by Bit: The National Curriculum at Key Stage 2* (Webb 1993) shows the following topics and their main subsidiary subject 'driver':

Autumn: Transport (science and geography);
Story telling (English and technology).

Spring: Invaders (history and English);
Healthy Living (science and geography).

If in one year topics focused on one subject more than others, the balance would be redressed in the next year.

Alongside plans for topic-related work, schools also often drew up plans for ongoing units of work across the core subjects, such as work following the school's mathematics scheme, music lessons with a specialist, and 'quiet reading' sessions. They also planned subject-focused 'mini-topics', to run parallel with the main class topic, covering subject-focused work that it was not easy to integrate into the class topics or special events such as a school Book Week or preparation for the Chinese New Year. Although topic-based planning remained very strong in primary schools, after the introduction of the National Curriculum teachers reported a move towards planning topics around subjects (Webb 1993) and a more widespread recognition that one integrated topic could not carry the whole curriculum, but that more than one form of planning was needed at any time.

Let us give an example of what a half-term topic might look like in practice in the key stage 1 classroom. In this example, our class teacher, who had a first degree in mathematics, planned his work within the frame of a whole school curriculum, drawing on the advice and support of the other curriculum subject specialists in the school. This half-term his main topic focus was the theme 'Growth and Change'. Having looked through the subject orders for his main focus, English, and his subsidiary focus, science (for this term), he drew up an outline of areas of the PoSs and ATs which he intended to focus on. He adapted his plans so that the starting-point reflected some of the current interests of the children in his class. One of them had talked about her new baby brother as the children sat in a circle on the carpet, sharing news. The other children had shown a lot of interest and had shared their own experience of babies. Some of them had gone on to write about babies they knew, drawing pictures and using a simple programme on the computer to write captions.

The teacher knew an older child in the school whose mother had just had a new baby. The mother agreed to bring the baby into the class regularly for a couple of months, so the children could see it growing and then record some of the ways in which it was changing. After watching the baby getting weighed, and helping to log the results on a wall chart (Maths AT14), the children asked the mother questions. She told them about the Baby Clinic she visited, and the children were fascinated. The teacher decided to turn the 'home corner' into a Baby Clinic. To structure their play he provided plenty of dolls, a variety of weighing scales, a 'changing table', and a baby bath. He also provided plenty of pencils and notepads for them to fill in their baby's records, and kept an 'appointments book' next to an old telephone for writing down 'appointments' (encouraging emergent writing).

The following week he was able to arrange for a small group to visit the Baby Clinic and report back to the class. Two bilingual children in the class reported that they had interviewed a doctor at the Clinic who turned out to share their languages, and, working together with the help of a bilingual support teacher, they developed an account of the conversation in English and Bengali on the class word-processor.

As the topic progressed, the teacher developed the theme to cover other subjects. In science, for example, under AT3, Processes of Life, at level 2 all primary children are expected to know that personal hygiene, food, exercise, rest and safety, and the proper and safe use of medicines are important; they are also expected to be able to give a similar account of the pattern of their own day. In AT1, Exploration of Science, children should be able to record findings in charts, drawings, and other appropriate forms.

The topic provided plenty of opportunity for the teacher to develop work in these areas. It was also linked to mathematics, where, for example, AT14, Handling Data, says pupils should help to design a data-collection sheet and use it to record a set of data leading to a frequency table. They should also construct, read, and interpret block graphs and frequency tables. As part of the history curriculum (AT1) the children and the teacher brought in photographs of themselves as babies, and produced their own 'time-lines' showing some of the changes that had happened to them from birth to 5 years old.

Indeed, the teacher found the problem was not finding ways to extend the topic out into different curriculum areas, but where to stop. He could, for example, have made a map of the route the class went on to visit the local Baby Clinic, bringing in geography as well. Teachers have continually to make decisions about how wide-ranging or restricted their topics should be, depending on their objectives at that time. The National Curriculum has been seen as offering help here:

Before, you didn't plan in the same detail as we plan now. I'm much more conscious of getting the balance between subjects . . . The problem with topics is that you have to decide what to leave out—perhaps we weren't selective enough before . . . that's why planning is so important, to have in your mind the areas of the curriculum that you want to cover and not to get side-tracked. (Head, quoted by Webb 1993)

Equally, not every aspect of the primary curriculum is covered by the National Curriculum subjects, and, through this topic, the teacher was able to pick up an important cross-curricular theme, health and safety. At the same time, he did not try to squeeze the whole curriculum into the topic. The whole school plan allowed him to make choices in the confidence that areas not covered this term would be picked up in the future.

However, he did add a self-contained unit of work around technology which was unconnected to the topic, as he wanted to provide experiences of using particular construction materials with one small group at a time to build up their skills in preparation for the next term's topic. He also planned a mini-topic over one week to follow up a poem the children had heard in assembly, bringing in dance and music. Teachers need to maintain enough flexibility in their plans to respond to their pupils' particular skills and needs, and to the unforeseen events that happen around them.

At secondary level, the same approach to planning is developed, although the starting-point is more likely to be through subjects.

Volcanoes and earthquakes: a secondary science project

Many people will remember studying volcanoes at school. It may have been in a science, geography, or even history lesson. Drawing a cross-section of an active volcano and hearing accounts of famous eruptions such as Krakatoa seem to stay long in most people's minds. The science statutory orders cover this through AT3. The statement of attainment at level 5 is: 'to be able to explain how earthquakes and volcanoes are associated with the formulation of landforms.' Here is an example of one approach to this subject.

The teacher has planned a series of lessons around the topic. The children begin by reading an account of the San Francisco earthquake of 1906, and the more recent one in 1989. They then use a slide sequence that describes the eruption of Vesuvius. This provides the starting-point for a run of activities planned around a chapter in the textbook that looks at volcanoes and earthquakes in the context of other attainment targets in science.

For example, pupils learn about the Richter scale for measuring the intensity of an earthquake, as set out in the second part of the statement of attainment for AT1, Exploration of Science: 'Select and use measuring-instruments to quantify variables and use more complex measuring instruments with the required degree of accuracy, for example, minor diversions on thermometers and force-meters.'

Schools plan the National Curriculum to maximize the cross-references that could be made to other subjects. The science teacher, for example, would be aware of English and mathematics attainment targets at level 5. The description of volcanic eruptions and earthquakes would develop English skills. Skills of data interpretation would be developed by looking at seismic graphs. The final part of this series of lessons is jointly taught by the class teachers of science and technology. The technology teacher has acquired a video that shows how high-rise buildings in places like San Francisco and Tokyo are constructed to withstand earth tremors and earthquakes.

4 Testing and Assessment

Testing and assessment is the issue that provokes the greatest controversy amongst educationists, parents, and the public generally. For pupils it can be one of the most worrying aspects of school life. It is also ultimately one of the most important. Tests, assessments, and examinations are a significant factor in determining job prospects or access to college or higher education. If you want to be a vet, the very highest grades at Advanced (A) level will be required. No one can become a teacher without obtaining General Certificates of Secondary Education (GCSE) in English and mathematics at grades A to C. A levels are also required.

The National Curriculum is accompanied by national assessments that begin at an early age. Previously, most pupils, apart from taking reading tests, were well into secondary schooling before they came into contact with a nationally standardized examination. Now a measurement is being made from the age of 7 about the progress that has been achieved. Many parents support this idea. This is not surprising, as most people expect some sort of feedback about how well their children are doing.

Immediately, however, problems begin to arise. Testing children to see how much they know appears to many people a straightforward process. In Chapter 2 the difficulty of monitoring standards was explained. Producing fair and reliable ways of testing children is equally difficult, and the government has spent millions of pounds on research projects in attempting to solve the problems.

Assessment is full of jargon, and before explaining the issues and methods being used, we need to define some of it. First, is there any difference between the terms 'tests', 'assessment', and 'examinations'? In practice the answer is no. All three terms are used interchangeably. Distinctions have begun to emerge, however, and in talking to teachers signs of this may be detected. Tests now tend to be seen as limited activities that contribute to the ongoing process of assessing. Examinations are usually seen as final, marking the end of the year or the end of the school process. Most commonly now they are associated with public examinations such as GCSEs or A levels. The term assessment, however, covers tests, examinations, and all the other ways in which teachers check and monitor progress.

The new approach to assessment

The sort of assessment that merely gives you a grade (like a formal public examination) tells you very little about which parts of the syllabus you did well on or where you went wrong. Giving you a position in a class list is much the same; all you can tell from the list is how you compare with others. The new approach to assessment attempts to do four things. First, it attempts to recognize when children have achieved a target, to acknowledge this in a positive way, and then to help them plan the next stages of learning. This is called *formative* assessment. Secondly, the assessment process aims to reveal weaknesses or difficulties in such a way that appropriate help can be given and the child can overcome the problem. This is termed the *diagnostic* purpose of assessment. This reflects the way most people learn. Initially learners experience patchy understanding. It is necessary to spot the areas of weakness and remedy them through extra work and attention. The driving test, for example, tries to be diagnostic in that you are given feedback on the specific parts of the test you fail. As you trek back sadly to your friendly instructor for further lessons, it would serve little purpose merely to announce that you had a D fail grade! The detailed recording and judgements involved in teachers' continuous assessment should, if working well, provide important formative and diagnostic information for every child. It is worth emphasizing that the aim is *to show the child what he or she has achieved*, not where they have failed!

Thirdly, the assessment process aims to give teachers, the child, and parents an overall summary of what has been achieved, at regular intervals. This is termed the *summative* purpose of assessment. In the National Curriculum the summary is made on the basis of levels of achievement in the attainment targets of the different subjects. This is discussed in greater detail later in the chapter. Fourthly, the results of these assessments are used by teachers, headteachers, and governors to see how well they are doing against the targets they will have established for the school as a whole. This could be called the *evaluative* purpose of assessment.

Reports on overall achievements for every school are made available to everyone in the form of public documents. More controversially the publication of National Curriculum assessment results at each key stage was proposed as a way of comparing individual school performance. By 1993 the interim report on the National Curriculum (DFE 1993) had highlighted the strength of feeling among teachers against using National Curriculum testing for the construction of performance tables. It also recommended that the approach to the measurement of school performance looked not only at 'the raw data of test or examination results but, rather, at the degree to which the school or college has helped the pupil to know and be able to do more: the extent to which it has added value'. At present the use of testing for this national evaluative purpose has been retained only for key stages 2 and 4, that is, at the end of the usual *primary* and *secondary* phases of education.

In the examples of classroom activities in Chapter 3 you will have seen how the teacher can use assessment for formative and diagnostic purposes. This is, of course, nothing new. The best teachers have always used a similar approach. The National Curriculum has given an added impetus to this, and in particular the chance to make assessment a positive experience for the child. Two further phrases help explain this more clearly.

The old system of assessment was almost wholly *norm referenced*, that is, pupils were placed in rank order and predetermined proportions were placed in the various grades. It implies that grades are assigned by comparison to other pupils' performance, rather than by the quality of the individual's performance. The idea of predetermined proportions was considered in Chapter 2. The 'bell curve' was, and in many examinations still is, used to allocate grades. The great difficulty with norm referencing is that a proportion of pupils are inevitably deemed to have done badly, and come away with a negative experience not only of the examination or test but of school generally.

The alternative to norm referencing is termed *criterion referencing*, and it is this that the National Curriculum assessments attempt to achieve. By this is meant a system where a pupil's achievements are judged in relation to specific objectives, irrespective of other pupils' performance. As we have seen, if the pupil shows competency against different statements of attainment then he or she will be deemed to have achieved success. The driving test is often used as an example of criterion referencing. Success or failure depends on a display of competency against specified criteria.

Categories of assessment

First, there is *continuous assessment* (also known as teacher assessment) by the teacher or teachers. This is the daily and weekly record in all aspects of the curriculum organized by the teacher and transferred on to individual record cards. Every so often the teacher will look at the detailed records of progress and make a judgement about the level of work being achieved by the child.

Secondly there are national tests. These are written and set outside the school by organizations commissioned by SCAA. Towards the end of a key stage children will complete a number of activities that will be marked and recorded to measure their level of attainment in a limited number of subjects. These tests will serve two purposes: first, in combination with the teacher assessments they will be used to report to parents and others the levels the children have reached in particular subjects at the end of each key stage. Secondly, by comparing the levels reached by children on these tests with the judgement being made by teachers through the continuous assessment process, it will be possible to check that teacher assessments are in line with nationally agreed standards.

Teachers use all sorts of ways of recording assessment continuously. They will take information from written work, from children's answers to questions, and from the way the children perform practical tasks individually or in a group. The national tests were originally intended to cover a similar range of activities, although by 1993 an emphasis was being placed on simpler, more manageable tests. It was hoped that by extensively trying out and piloting these tasks with hundreds of children they would give reliable information about the level children can achieve.

The nature of the assessment tasks, their purpose in the assessment of children, and the relationship between teacher assessment and national tests continued to be the subject of intense debate. The review completed at the end of 1993 made it very clear that the task of assessing the national curriculum had become too bureaucratic. The report was particularly insistent that teachers need not keep elaborate tick lists for every attainment target at every level:

Records supplement the teacher's personal and professional knowledge of a child. It is not possible for teachers to record all their knowledge and they should not be tempted to try. Written records complement this professional understanding. If record systems do not provide a significant contribution to teaching and learning there is little point in maintaining them.

Records of children's attainments are likely to contain details that will inform reports to parents. Records that are over-detailed or complex tend to hinder rather than support this task. They should help identify clearly the child's strengths, weaknesses and progress for parents and provide information that will indicate the next steps forward for the child.

(Dearing, R., 1993)

How continuous assessment works

Teachers are unable to assess all the children in their class all the time. Throughout the year, therefore, it is likely that they will give particular attention to two or three children at a time. This is known as a 'rolling programme'. In the last section we saw some primary teaching focusing initially on AT1, Speaking and Listening, and AT3, Writing. In continuously assessing, the teacher could on one day:

- have individual conversations with four or five children to see that they could briefly describe an event from the previous day. The teacher will be experienced in judging whether the child is confident in doing this (in which case a note will be made in the child's record) or whether further practice is needed (in which case the teacher may suggest an activity in the group where the child can practise further). The teacher would also make a mental (or perhaps written) note to have another conversation later in the week in which an event can be described briefly.

- after school, spend some time looking at the written work completed by all the children. The teacher would be looking, for example, for evidence of sentences with capital letters and full stops; and simple, coherent non-chronological writing. AT3 at level 2 includes this as a statement of attainment that all children should strive towards. As she looked at the books the teacher would make a note against each child's record. It is unlikely that a judgement would be made about whether the child would be fully competent on the basis of one piece of written work. The teacher will have built up a knowledge of each child over the year and will use a variety of evidence in making a final assessment.

The secondary science teacher working on rocks and soil will be involved in a similar process.

- In this class the teacher is using a recording system that allows her to note when pupils are successful with practical activities. In science classes today there are few occasions on which all children are asked to do the same activity, then stop and wait to have their work marked by the teacher. More commonly they carry out investigations and the teacher observes different parts of the process to see how well they are doing. During one week's lessons, therefore, the teacher may observe all the groups and make judgements about pupils' competency in choosing and using appropriate measuring instruments with a reasonable degree of accuracy (AT1, Scientific Investigation, level 4).
- In the same class the teacher may set a written assignment, following reading and discussion in class, that provides evidence of the child's understanding of different weathering processes that lead to different soil types (AT3 level 4). The teacher's written comments in the children's exercise books would indicate how well they had done and how, if necessary, they could go over the work again (or follow it up in a different way) to achieve a fresh understanding of the concept. Depending on how well the group as a whole had done, the teacher could decide: (1) to do something with the whole class on this, (2) to follow up the concept with a group of pupils, or (3) to give some individual help as the vast majority had clearly grasped what was involved.

Every so often teachers will take their records and make judgements about the level being achieved against each of the attainment targets they are covering. This is the information used to produce the annual report to parents, which includes details on teacher assessment results and national test results (in the final year of a key stage), as well as all the other information about how hard their child is working, whether he or she seem to be enjoying the subject, how regularly homework is being completed, and so forth. The right to receive an annual report on their child's progress and the opportunity to discuss it with a teacher is set out in the Parent's Charter and subsequent legislation on assessment, recording, and reporting. Parents may also wish to ask about the sort of recording system being used daily. Schools will be explaining this at parents' evenings or at special events to describe the way the National Curriculum works in practice. Each school has established its own record scheme, following advice from national organizations like SCAA as well as from local advisers or inspectors.

The national tests

In the National Curriculum tests made up of standard assessment tasks (SATs) have been developed to measure individual achievement against specified criteria. The acronym SATs has now entered into educational folklore. Through most of the early part of the 1990s different groups of people, including university departments, publishers, and private organizations, have been beavering away trying to develop valid and reliable assessments or SATs against which the accuracy of the teacher's assessment can be measured. It has proved an extremely difficult and complex task, and many strong criticisms have been made of some of the first attempts. For example, some SATs have provided what appears to be accurate information about children's progress, but in so doing have produced bewilderingly detailed information for parents. On the other hand, where simple information has been produced, the validity and reliability have been called into question. Part of the problem for the early SATs appears to lie with a lack of clarity as to their function. In the early pilots, many of the tasks were attempting to provide diagnostic, formative, and summative assessment information. These complex assessments were criticized as taking up too much time for completing and marking, and adding little new information to the teachers' assessments. SATs were then seen to be taking up valuable teaching time and adding further work to an already administratively overloaded profession. However, when the nature of the tasks was changed to more simple 'pencil and paper' tests, these were criticized as unsuitable for testing the processes and skills dimension of the National Curriculum.

By 1993 three years of mandatory national tests had been carried out at key stage 1 in English, mathematics, and science. Pilot testing had also been carried out for these same subjects at key stage 3 in 1991 and 1992. However, 1993 saw a national campaign led by teachers' and parents' associations, drawing attention to the overload in the curriculum and the unmanageability of the national testing arrangements. The mandatory tests due to take place in 1993 were severely disrupted by teachers' industrial action.

The review of the National Curriculum has led to significant changes. It recognized that the assessment had been far too complex and time-consuming and that continued efforts should be made to shorten and simplify the assessments carried out by teachers and the national tests. The decision, accepted by the government was

- in Key Stage 1, tests would be in English and maths only, with the total test time for pupils cut by half, and science covered by teacher assessment;
- the Key Stage 2 tests would be treated as a voluntary national pilot;
- in Key Stage 3, the overall test time for pupils would be cut by half.

Particular emphasis is now given to teachers visiting other schools and comparing the judgements they are making with others in the locality. This process of moderation, common practice in the exam year of the secondary school, is becoming increasingly common in the primary and lower secondary years.

The ten-level scale

The original plan was to introduce the ten-level scale right across the compulsory years of 5–16. This has now been abandoned and the scale only applies to Key Stages 1–3. The strengths of the system have been in the way it charts progression from 5 to 16, and is therefore a national scale readily understood by parents and teachers to chart progress and continuity throughout the years of schooling.

However, four major problems have been identified:

1. In using this scale some 1,000 statements of attainment have been produced. This has proved difficult to manage in terms of assessing children, and many would argue that knowledge, understanding, and skill cannot be divided into neat packages in this way.

2. Except in mathematics the levels are not tied to particular programmes of study. This has led to problems such as: is the level 3 that a 6-year-old is working on for a key stage 1 topic comparable to that of a 9-year-old working on a different key stage 2 topic?

3. The gap between some levels is so large that pupils can stay working at that level for a long time. This may have an impact on motivation. It also suggests that differentiating between children working at the same level is not adequate.

4. Higher levels of attainment involve selecting and synthesizing knowledge, skills, and understanding. Requires a different approach to teaching and learning from that suggested by individual statements of attainment.

Changes in the use of the scale through the mid-1990s are likely and it is wise to obtain information from schools about the latest way in which the levels are being interpreted both by teachers and in the national tests.

The slimming-down of the National Curriculum will have profound effects on the assessment system. These changes will be implemented, however, after September 1995 when the revised curriculum is introduced into schools. The revision of each subject order into a statutory core and optional studies to be taught at the discretion of the teacher will have an enormous impact on the future scale of testing; as will the reduction in the number of statements of attainment on which teachers have to make judgements.

Records of achievement

Alongside teachers' continuous assessment, SATs, and the GCSE, there has been another development that has had an impact on a great many schools. *Records of achievement* were first planned in the 1970s and early 1980s, to give much greater acknowledgement to what young people achieved in school. Originally this began in secondary schools, where the vast majority of school leavers had very little to show for their efforts and enthusiasm across the broad range of school life. Examination results gave an indication of academic attainment, but what about all the other qualities that schools have a responsibility to develop?

Achievements in creative activities, the school play or other aspects of drama, music, and dance gained little recognition. Sporting achievement may have gained passing recognition, but there was no ongoing record that the pupils could take away with them. And then there are the host of other pursuits that the good school fosters: outdoor pursuits, community help programmes, and charity fund-raising, to give just three examples. Only in a very few schools had these been systematically recorded.

By the late 1980s a great many schools were using a 'record of achievement'. The form and style varied from area to area, but most aimed to record achievements in all aspects of school life. Some also recorded important achievements outside school. In 1995 all children will leave school with a National Record of Achievement. The pupil usually works with a form teacher or counsellor to compile and collate the research. The records contain information about academic work as well, including grades obtained in examinations. Achievements on the way to public examinations are as important as the final grades, and nearly all records of achievement recognize this. Many young people choose to use their record at interviews with potential employers or when transferring to other forms of education. It is also a document to be kept at home, treasured, and years later shown with some pride to the grandchildren!

The 1988 Education Reform Act does make some aspects of assessment statutory, and it is important to note these. Section 4 (2) of the Education Reform Act allows the Secretary of State to specify attainment targets and programmes of study in the National Curriculum. At other places in the Act there is specific reference to assessment, records, and reporting. The plans for how schools are to implement the reformed system are now in the Act, but are contained in orders and regulations issued by the Secretary of State following discussion and consultation. There is now a clear requirement for schools to give an annual report to parents on the progress being made by their child. This will involve information about levels achieved, backed up by a written report. The school will need to support this with a personal interview. The teacher-training materials produced by SEAC (now SCAA) strongly advocated a collaborative approach between parents and teachers in reviewing the work of the child. Parents, they point out, should 'have access to the detailed picture of the child's progress, of where the progress is rapid and where that progress is slow. Sensitively handled, there is an excellent opportunity for the creation of a helpful and supportive relationship between teacher, parent and pupil.' The way class and school assessments are reported is explained in Chapter 8, which looks in more detail at parents and the National Curriculum.

To summarize, therefore, National Curriculum assessments include both teacher assessments and national tests. They are intended to be very different from the kind of tests most adults experienced at school. They should:

- give credit for hard work and achievement;
- point out gaps or weaknesses that, independently or with the teacher, can be remedied;
- indicate realistically what can be attempted next;
- record an individual's specific attainments and performance.

Parents will receive plenty of guidance from teachers and schools about how to interpret the increased variety of information available to them.

5 The Core Foundation Subjects: English, Mathematics, and Science

The core foundation subjects have been revised since the introduction of the National Curriculum in 1988. Further revisions will be considered in 1994 and new statutory orders will take effect from September 1995. The descriptions below describe the background to the way the subject is taught today in the context of the existing national curriculum framework for each subject.

English

The working group that devised the English programme of study and attainments targets in England structured their thinking around five models of English. Brian Cox described these as:

1 a 'personal growth' view, focuses on the child: it emphasises the relationship between language and learning in the individual child, and the role of literature in developing children's imaginative and aesthetic lives;

2 a 'cross-curricular' view focuses on the school: it emphasises that all teachers have a responsibility to help children with the language demands of different subjects on the school curriculum. In England, English is different from other school subjects, in that it is both a subject and a medium of instruction for other subjects;

3 an 'adult-needs' view focuses on communication outside the school: it emphasises the responsibility of English teachers to prepare children for the language demands of adult life, including the workplace, in a fast-changing world. Children need to learn to deal with day-to-day demands of spoken language and of print; they also need to be able to write clearly, appropriately and effectively;

4 a 'cultural heritage' view emphasises the responsibility of schools to lead children to an appreciation of those works of literature that have been widely regarded as amongst the finest in the language;

5   a 'cultural analysis' view emphasises the role of English in helping children towards a critical understanding of the world and cultural environment in which they live. Children should know about the processes by which meanings are conveyed, and about the ways in which print and other media carry values. (Cox 1991: 21–2)

The working group translated these five models of English into the Report on the English curriculum in schools, which was to provide a 'broad and balanced curriculum', and to ensure that all pupils' learning should be planned so that progression and continuity were ensured. The Report was to be organized around two central structures: attainment targets and programmes of study.

Attainment targets

The working group devised five attainment targets:

AT1. Speaking and Listening; AT2. Reading; AT3. Writing; AT4. Spelling; AT5. Handwriting.

The working group decided to organize these five attainment targets into three areas; Speaking and Listening, Reading, and Writing, which incorporated ATs 4 and 5. 'We chose these three components because this division of the English Curriculum would be familiar to English teachers and in accord with good practice' (Cox 1991: 10). All the areas were seen as interrelated. An English teacher may choose to highlight reading, but inevitably the lessons will also involve the pupils in both writing and speaking and listening.

An extract from the attainment targets at key stage 1 in Speaking and Listening at level 1 shows that pupils should be able to:

participate as speakers and listeners in group activities, including imaginative play.

Example: Suggest what to do next in a practical activity; tell stories; play the role of shopkeeper or customer in the class shop.

By the end of key stage 2 (7–11) at level 4 in Speaking and Listening, pupils should be able to:

take part as speakers and listeners in a group discussion or activity, expressing a personal view and commenting constructively on what is being discussed or experienced.

Example: Draft a piece of writing, with others, on a word-processor; contribute to the planning and implementation of a group activity.

At the end of key stage 3 (11–14), level 6 pupils should be able to:

> contribute to group discussions considered opinions or clear statements of personal feeling which are clearly responsive to the contributions of others.
>
> *Example*: Present or develop a line of reasoning in discussion of an issue raised by a story and comment on other viewpoints.

By key stage 4 (14–16) at level 7 pupils should be able to:

> express a point of view clearly and cogently to a range of audiences and interpret accurately a range of statements by others.
>
> *Example*: Present a personal opinion or a belief to younger pupils, another teacher, or another adult.

Pupils achieving level 10 could:

> express a point of view on complex subjects persuasively, cogently, and clearly, applying and interpreting a range of methods of presentation and assessing their own effectiveness accurately.
>
> *Example*: Devise and mount an advertising campaign concerned with a matter of principle.

We can see from these extracts that the National Curriculum attainment targets require an increasing complexity of skills from pupils as they progress through the levels. Yet one of the difficulties of organizing the curriculum in this way is the nature of learning: pupils rarely learn in this neat, linear way. Rather, learning is recursive: there are times of great progress, followed by a period of consolidation, or even some falling back. However, whilst recognizing this, the statements of attainment indicate how pupils' progress in English can be recorded.

Programmes of study

The programmes of study are in key stages. Each key stage begins with general provisions, which provide overall guidelines indicating progress, and detailed provisions, which indicate specific issues pupils should be working on in order to achieve particular levels.

So, for example, programmes of study for key stage 2 include in general provisions that:

> The reading materials provided should include a range of fiction, non-fiction, and poetry, as well as periodicals suitable for children of this age. These should include works written in English from other cultures. School and class libraries must provide as wide a range as possible. Pupils should discuss with others and with the teacher what has been read.

Detailed provisions indicate that:

> In order to achieve level 4, pupils should be taught how to use lists of contents, indexes, databases, a library classification system, and catalogues to select information.

AT key stages 3 and 4, general provisions indicate that pupils should, for example:

- use the evidence in a text to interpret and form judgements about characters' motives and be able to quote evidence in support of their views;
- be shown how to recognize that the attitudes and behaviour of a character or narrator are not necessarily the attitudes or beliefs of the author.

Detailed provisions indicate that, in order to achieve level 8, pupils should be taught how to:

- scrutinize a text for details of characterization, settings, and attitudes;
- quote accurately from a text to support their opinions;
- recognize the author's viewpoint and—where relevant—persuasive or rhetorical techniques in a range of texts.

Strands

If we imagine the National Curriculum in English organized as a matrix, we have as one axis the ten levels of attainment in each attainment target (Speaking and Listening, Reading, and Writing). The other axis is formed by strands: the skills of each attainment target grouped together. This organizational principle was to support both planning and assessment in the classroom. The following charts (Speaking and Listening, Reading, and Writing) show how these strands operate in the English National Curriculum:

Speaking and Listening:
   Strand 1: Personal;
   Strand 2: Information/Explanation;
   Strand 3: Performance;
   Strand 4: Collaboration/Discussion;
   Strand 5: Knowledge about Language.

Reading:
   Strand 1: Fluency and Range;
   Strand 2: Response;
   Strand 3: Media and Non-literary;
   Strand 4: Study Skills;
   Strand 5: Knowledge about Language.

Writing:
   Strand 1: Structure/Organization;
   Strand 2: Variety/Audience;
   Strand 3: Style;
   Strand 4: Drafting;
   Strand 5: Knowledge about Language.

Knowledge about language

Teaching about language is, in broad terms, not a new departure for most English teachers. However, treating knowledge about language systematically and giving it explicit mention in the syllabus is not universal in English departments in England and Wales. (English 5–16: s. 6.1)

One strand which runs through all of the three profile components is knowledge about language (KAL). The following chart shows how KAL is integrated into all three profile components.

Statements of attainment in knowledge about language

In the Speaking and Listening profile component pupils should be able to achieve the following standards at levels 5–10:

5. talk about variations in vocabulary between different regional or social groups, e.g. dialect vocabulary, specialist terms;

6. talk about some grammatical differences between spoken Standard English and a non-standard variety;
7. talk about appropriateness in the use of spoken language, according to purpose, topic, and audience, e.g. differences between language appropriate to a job interview and to a discussion with peers;
8. talk about the contribution that facial expressions, gestures, and tone of voice can make to a speaker's meaning, e.g. in ironic and sarcastic uses of language;
9. talk about ways in which language varies between different types of spoken communication, e.g. joke, anecdote, conversation, commentary, lecture;
10. talk about some of the factors that influence people's attitudes to the way other people speak.

In the Writing profile component, pupils should be able to:

5. talk about variations in vocabulary according to purpose, topic, and audience and according to whether language is spoken or written, e.g. slang, formal vocabulary, technical vocabulary;
6. demonstrate some knowledge of straightforward grammatical differences between spoken and written English;
7. comment on examples of appropriate and inappropriate use of language in written texts, with respect to purpose, topic, and audience;
8. demonstrate some knowledge of organizational differences between spoken and written English;
9. demonstrate some knowledge of ways in which language varies between different types of written text, e.g. personal letter, formal letter, printed instructions, newspaper report, play script;
10. demonstrate some knowledge of criteria by which different types of written language can be judged, e.g. clarity, coherence, accuracy, appropriateness, effectiveness, vigour, etc.

In the Reading profile component pupils should be able to:

5. recognize and talk about the use of word play, e.g. puns, unconventional spellings, etc., and some of the effects of the writer's choice of words in imaginative uses of English;

6. talk about examples (from their own experience or from their reading) of changes in word use and meaning over time, and about some of the reasons for these changes, e.g. technological developments, euphemism, contact with other languages, fashion;

7. talk about some of the effects of sound patterning, e.g. rhyme, alliteration, and figures of speech, e.g. similes, metaphors, personification, in imaginative uses of English;

8. identify in their reading, and talk and write about, some of the changes in the grammar of English over time, e.g. in pronouns (from *thou* and *thee* to *you*), in verb forms, in negatives, etc.;

9. demonstrate some understanding of the use of special lexical and grammatical effects in literary language, e.g. the repetition of words or structures, dialect forms, archaisms, grammatical deviance, etc.;

10. demonstrate some understanding of attitudes in society towards language change and of ideas about appropriateness and correctness in language use.

The working group was clear that knowledge about language was a highly significant part of the English curriculum.

Two justifications for teaching pupils explicitly about language are, firstly, the positive effect on aspects of their use of language, and secondly, the general value of such knowledge as an important part of their understanding of their social and cultural environment, since language has vital functions in the life of the individual and of society. (English 5–16: s. 6.7)

However, knowledge about language was also an area which generated some of the liveliest debates in English, specifically concerning recommendations over Standard English and the teaching of grammar. Newspapers could not agree over the implications of the recommendations (see Figs. 4–6).

Standard English is defined by the working group as 'a dialect of English' (s. 5.42), with the understanding that dialect refers to 'grammar and vocabulary, but not to accent' (s. 4.9). That all pupils should 'learn, and if necessary be explicitly taught, Standard English' (s. 4.4) is justified by reference to its widespread use in 'the education system and in professional life, in public and formal uses, and in writing and particularly in print' (s. 4.9). The working group present Standard

Victory to Baker

Schools must teach all pupils to speak and write standard English

By STEPHEN BATES, Education Correspondent

KENNETH BAKER has won his battle to make sure all pupils leave school with a firm grasp of grammar and standard English.

Educationalists yesterday bowed to his demands that children must be taught how to speak properly and write clearly.

They said all must be able to speak and write in standard English: write clearly, neatly and grammatically: spell correctly and read the great works of English literature, especially Shakespeare.

Pupils must leave school knowing how to judge information from sources like the media, and how to stand up for their rights and complain articulately as consumers.

Senior officials said the new report on how English is to be taught under the Government's national curriculum had given the Education Secretary all he wanted.

Mr Baker himself said: 'Grammar and standard English have a key place. So do literature—including poetry and drama—and information technology and media education, which are becoming increasingly important in adult life.'

'Next year the national curriculum core subjects of science, mathematics and English will be firmly in place.

That will be a milestone in levering up standards in our schools.' The report, by a working party of the National Curriculum Council lays down what should be learned by pupils from seven to 16 in England and Wales.

An earlier report on what should be taught to five to seven-year-olds caused a furore for downgrading grammar and claiming that sloppy English was 'rarely more than a social irritant'.

Mr Baker insisted that primary schools should teach grammar and spelling and introduce pupils to poetry and literature.

This report spells out much more clearly that as an international language, standard English must be taught to all pupils, even if not at the expense of their local accents and dialects, and that they must leave school knowing how and when to speak it.

It rejects the idea of old-fashioned rote grammar learning, and drops a controversial suggested reading list which omitted favourite children's authors like Enid Blyton.

But it recommends that all pupils must have had a chance to read the classics.

From 11, teachers should introduce pupils to some of the works that have been most influential in shaping and refining the English language and its literature—for example the Authorised Version of the Bible, Wordsworth's poems or Dickens's novels.

In particular they should give pupils the opportunity to gain some experience of the works of Shakespeare.

The report says pupils need to be articulate to get jobs and should be given lessons in speaking and listening.

They should have drama lessons at primary school and parents should encourage children to enjoy books.

The report now goes out to consultation and is likely to be implemented for seven and 11-year-olds from September 1990 and for 14-year-olds in September 1992.

LISTEN AND LEARN

At SEVEN, most pupils should be able to convey a simple message and listen attentively to stories and poems, says the working party's report. They should also be able to read aloud and silently; write in complete sentences using capital letters, full stops and question marks; spell simple words correctly; begin clear and legible joined-up writing; tell stories and recite simple poems by heart.

SPELLING IT OUT

At 11, they should be able to describe an event and discuss a point of view; take part in a scene from a play; read and discuss books, stories and poems of different sorts. They should also be able to write in standard English; spell words correctly; write clearly and legibly and be able to recognise different forms of English including dialects, slang and puns.

OPINION FORMERS

By 14, they should be able to express opinions on complex subjects; read and discuss a range of poetry, fiction, non-fiction and drama; understand grammatical differences and write organised essays; write fluently and legibly; recognise complex spellings. At 16, give a presentation, listen critically, be self-critical about arguments and read wide-ranging works of literature.

Fig. 4　*Daily Mail* Report

English as the language of wider communication, and as such its teaching becomes an issue of access. The controversy arises over the social prestige of Standard English (which is why it is often, but wrongly, confused with received pronunciation. Standard English can be spoken with any accent). The extensive use of Standard English in public life has led to it often being seen as superior to non-standard, or regional, dialects. The difference actually lies in the vocabulary and sentence syntax (construction) of Standard English having been elaborated, whereas those of non-standard dialects, for social and historical reasons, have not. Creole varieties of English (for example, Black British English and Patois) should also be recognized as having their own complex and rule-governed structure, and not

Baker defeated on grammar

By CELIA WESTON

MR KENNETH BAKER, the Education Secretary, yesterday conceded that the Government cannot force schools to adopt his preference for formal grammar teaching.

He has also had to admit defeat on emphasising reading and writing as more important than speaking and listening in the teaching of English, one of the three core subjects of the national curriculum.

Mr Baker has endorsed the final report of the working party on English teaching, chaired by Professor Brian Cox. The report was published yesterday by the Department of Education and Science.

Mr Baker said that literature—including poetry and drama—information technology and media education also had a key place in English. Next year the two other core subjects of mathematics and science would also be in place in schools. He said it was a 'milestone in levering up standards in our schools'.

The report steers a course between strict grammarians, favoured by Mr Baker, and more informal schools of thought. It goes to great lengths to justify not coming down on either side of the argument and its proposals signal defeat for Mr Baker after a public row last year on the formal teaching of grammar and Standard English in primary schools.

For primary school children, compromise proposals, which will be implemented from September, included teaching children about grammatical terms. But Mr Baker's call to make grammar central to teaching the language was rejected.

The report on English teaching says that in the last 20 years 'grammatical drills and sentence parsing have come to be recognised as being mostly mechanical and uninteresting.' But pupils should be taught more or less explicit grammatical analysis in order to interpret texts and write accurately.

It says all pupils should learn to speak and write Standard English competently because it served as a language of wider communication.

But the aim was to add Standard English to a child's repertoire, not to replace other dialects and languages.

The National Association for the Teaching of English welcomed the report as a broad consensus which would be widely accepted by teachers. It was particularly pleased by the emphasis on speaking and listening and because the vital interaction of language and literature was fully recognised.

The National Union of Teachers, however, warned that a shortage of English teachers could prevent the proposals being put into practice.

Consultation on the proposals will end in September. The programme for 11 and 14-year-olds will begin in autumn 1990 and for 16-year-olds in 1992 when more work has been done to reconcile the demands of the national curriculum with the GCSE.

Fig. 5 *Guardian* Report

By ROBERT BOLTON

TEACHERS no longer need to correct the bad grammar of pupils, a new report on English claimed yesterday.

The top-level document, backed by Education Secretary Kenneth Baker, says teachers have 'little hope' of changing the way children speak.

It adds: 'There is little point in correcting the spoken language of pupils in any general way.'

But last night Tory MP Sir Rhodes Boyson slammed the report's conclusions.

He said: 'Teachers should be putting across proper English and expect to be spoken to in the same way by children.

'Grammar has to be taught. It is not something children are born with.'

Sir Rhodes, a former headmaster, added: 'Standard English is the pass–port to mobility.

'Sloppiness in speech rules you out for a job.

WOOLLY

'One of the reasons why we are so bad at foreign languages is because we don't know the grammar of our own language.'

The report, produced by a 10-strong committee, states that children should know when to use proper English.

It adds: 'They should recognise that "we was, he ain't, they never" are not grammatical.'

The report was 'beefed up' after Mr Baker complained that an earlier version was 'too woolly.'

It will be sent to head teachers, school governors and parents for their views.

Fig. 6   *Sun* Report

---

seen as simplified variations of Standard English. In addition, Standard English itself changes with time and use. However, the National Curriculum is clear that it is the entitlement of all pupils to learn Standard English, but that 'The aim is to add Standard English to the repertoire [of pupils], not to replace the other dialects or languages' (s. 4.43). The working group was also clear on approaches to teaching Standard English for writing and for speaking.

- there is little point in correcting the spoken language of pupils in any general way . . . because it is unlikely to have a beneficial effect. Moreover, criticism of pupils' spoken language will be interpreted as criticism of their family and friends;
- if teachers concentrate on pupils' competence in written Standard English, pupils will gain sufficient knowledge of Standard English to be able to convert this into competence in spoken Standard English when appropriate.

In general terms, the working group recommended that explicit teaching about the nature and functions of Standard English should begin in the upper years of the primary school; that by year 7 pupils should be using Standard English in written work; that secondary schools should provide opportunities where spoken Standard English would be appropriate to the occasion; and that by year 10 all pupils should be able to choose to use Standard English in speech when appropriate.

The teaching of grammar inspires the same level of debate. Grammar is often understood to mean the 'correct use of the standard language' (s, 4.17), and again much of the controversy stems from this fundamental misapprehension of the term grammar. Linguists distinguish between prescriptive grammar ('the view that it is possible to lay down rules for the correct use of language', s. 4.18), and descriptive grammar ('the view that the way people actually use language should be accurately described, without prescription of how they ought to use it', s. 4.19). The working group did not see these as mutually exclusive: 'We must recognise that we need both accurate descriptions of language that are related to situation, purpose and mode . . . and prescriptions that take account of context, appropriateness and the expression of meaning' (Cox 1991: 35). The perceived 'rejection' of grammar teaching was based on the recommendation of the Kingman Report (an inquiry into English teaching published in 1988) of 'no return to old-fashioned grammar teaching' (s. 4.24). But this was because the latter was seen as an inadequate account of the English language (Kingman Report 1988: ch. 1, para. 11). Instead, the working group recommended that, for grammar to be of relevance to English teaching, it should be:

- a form of grammar which can describe English in use;
- relevant to all levels from the syntax of sentences through to the organisation of substantial texts;
- able to describe the considerable differences between written and spoken English;
- part of a wider syllabus of language study. (English 5–16: s. 4.28)

Teaching grammar has not then been abandoned by English teachers; in fact, quite the opposite. The concept has been widened to look at how language works, and English teachers are concerned to ensure that teaching about language is made relevant and immediate to their pupils.

These two major areas in English teaching have been discussed to give an indication of the kinds of debates in the field. There are others: approaches to literature, including discussions over the canon of literature (that is, recommended texts for use in schools); the balance on assessment between coursework set and marked in school, and external examinations; whether reading is taught through the use of phonics ('sounding out') or 'real books'. These and other issues are likely to be the subject of ongoing debate.

Assessment

Assessment in English has been through a number of stages of trial and development at all key stages. The key stage tests, now known as national tests, were first trialled, and then piloted on a staged basis. KS1 was piloted in 1990, with the first statutory tests administered in 1991. An example of the reading section of the KS1 test is reproduced below. The example is taken from the 1994 tests.

KS 2 and KS3 were piloted in 1992. In 1994 KS2 tests were at the stage of the first optional national pilot, with the first statutory years predicted for 1995, but dependent on the Dearing review. When KS3 tests were first piloted in 1993 they were not thought by the government to be successful, and a new format was designed. These tests were organized in tiers, with pupils below level 3 being teacher-assessed only and pupils above level 3 being entered by their teachers at the appropriate tier for the test. The test itself was based around a written comprehension and questions on an anthology of literature, which was distributed to all schools. These tests were

SoA

Show signs of a developing interest in reading

Talk in simple terms about the content of stories, or information in non-fiction books

Recognise that print is used to carry meaning, in books and in other forms in the everyday world

Begin to recognise individual words or letters in familiar contexts

Evidence of Attainment

① Chooses a book and talks about it, or shows interest by non-verbal means

① Talks about the content of the book (story or characters or pictures). More is expected than answers to the teacher's questions

① Shows understanding that print carries meaning

① Recognises at least one word and at least three letters

Resources

You will need a selection of books suitable for beginner readers.

What to do

• Ask the child to choose a familiar book and to tell you the reasons for the choice

This activity should be introduced so that the child is relaxed and feels free to talk about the choice of books. Offer books that are familiar; the child should have heard them read aloud on a number of occasions and should know them quite well.

There is no need to use any particular wording in your conversation. Satisfy yourself that the child is showing interest in books by talking about the choice or by other, non-verbal means.

• Ask the child to tell you about the book.

Encourage the child to look through the book, telling you as much as possible. Follow up any comments and ask open questions such as *Can you tell me anything else?* or *What happens next?*

To demonstrate evidence of attainment, a child is not required to retell the contents of the book in full, but should make at least one comment about the story, the characters, favourite events or pictures.

• Ask *Where does it tell me what to say?* or *How do I know what to read?*	There is no need to use this exact wording; the point of this activity is to find out whether the child understands that it is the print – the letters and the words – which tells the reader what to read (rather than thinking, for example, that the reader looks at the pictures and makes up the words).
• Ask the child to pick out some words and to point out or say some letters (names or sounds)	Choose significant words in the book, perhaps a word from the title, or the name of the main character. Ask about several different letters in order to satisfy yourself that the child has identified at least three correctly.

KS1 (Reading), 1994

due to be nationally administered in 1993. However, English teachers were not in agreement with this format, and the 1993 tests were in the main not administered by schools. The tests were redesigned for 1994. The 1994 tests were to assess levels 4–7, with an extension paper for levels 8–10. Pupils below level 4 were to be teacher-assessed. The two papers were comprehension and essay, with spelling and handwriting assessed, and a Shakespeare paper on prescribed scenes from set plays. The following extracts are from the sample papers distributed to schools in October 1993.

Section C

7   Write on **one** of the following topics.

   (*a*)   'Making my Mind Up' or 'The Wrong Decision.'
   You may find it helpful to present your writing in a particular form, for example a story, an article or a letter to a friend. You may use the ideas and characters from the reading-passages as a starting-point for your writing if you wish.

   (*b*)   A description or story about your life in ten years' time. You could either write this realistically or imagine that all your dreams have come true.

   (*c*)   Do you think it is better to be an individual or to be like everyone else? Write your views on this. If you wish, you could write this as a letter to the newspaper, replying to the article in Section A.

ROMEO AND JULIET
Act 3 Scene 1

TASK

Imagine you are a bystander who saw everything that happened in this scene and who knows what led up to it.

Explain, to a friend who has only heard the outline of what went on, what you think were the most significant moments in the scene. Was the treatment of Romeo fair and just? Refer to what the characters said and did in this scene and earlier in the play to support your view.

To help you   In deciding what to write, you may find it helpful to think about the following:

- what led up to these events;
- the most dramatic moments for anyone watching;
- the words and actions of Mercutio, Tybalt and Romeo, and what you already know about these characters;
- the Prince's verdict, the options open to him and your view of his decision.

The extension paper asks pupils to compare extracts from two texts, and then to produce some personal writing using the ideas of the two texts as starting-points.

At KS4 the debate centred around the balance between assessment by externally marked examination papers and internally marked coursework. Claims for the former centred around the need for objectivity in testing, and for the latter, that it gave pupils opportunities to display a wide range of abilities over a period of time, and to be assessed by teachers who knew the pupils and their capabilities. The coursework element, which with some exam boards had been 100 per cent, was reduced to 40 per cent, 20 per cent of which had to be used in assessing speaking and listening.

The national curriculum orders for English and the assessment arrangements were applicable to both England and Wales. In Northern Ireland, both the orders and the assessment arrangements are different.

Northern Ireland

The Northern Ireland English curriculum is based on three principles:

- English is heuristic: to do with discovery;
- English is recursive: development is often charted not by the acquisition of new skills but by a more sophisticated ability to handle familiar ones;
- English is holistic: the four modes of language are inextricably interwoven (English Guidance materials NICC 1990).

Broadly, the English curriculum covers KAL, literature, drama, and media education within mutually supportive and flexible programmes of study. The PoS cater for all pupils regardless of attainment, gender, race, or religion. There are three attainment targets: Talking and Listening, Reading, and Writing. Although the statements of attainment are different from those of the England and Wales orders, the framework for the summative assessment is still based on TGAT. The reported outcomes in terms of subject levels are therefore equivalent. In Northern Ireland the key stage tests are not known as national tests, but as CAIs—common assessment instruments. In 1993 the CAIs piloted took the form of assessment units. These units in both reading and writing were written by NISEAC (Northern Ireland Schools Examination and Assessment Council) to be administered in schools by teachers of English. The assessment units are chosen by the teacher from a catalogue of assessment units, at the level the teacher thinks appropriate to that pupil. Each pupil must attempt at least one unit in reading and one in writing. These units each require 20–30 minutes' individual work from the pupil and are available for the teacher to use when he or she feels it is appropriate. There are no timetabled, written tests and no external marking. The Library Boards, which are the equivalent of LEAs, moderate the results.

Mathematics

Mathematics is one of the three core subjects in the National Curriculum. The mathematics working group, reporting its proposal for the National Curriculum, suggested that mathematics has such status because 'it provides a means for organising, communicating and manipulating information, and has the ability to suggest possible answers to practical problems' (DES/WO 1988: 2.1).

In defining a National Curriculum for mathematics the group examined the mathematical needs of adult life so that the mathematics taught in school should reflect the skills that pupils would need later on, and especially the needs of industry and commerce.

They consulted recent surveys and in particular focused on the demand for the traditional basic arithmetic skills. In many instances they found these to be increasingly undertaken by calculators and computers. While recognizing the need for facility with the four rules of number, the emphasis on the skills of long division and long multiplication could be reduced and 'the time saved can be used to improve standards of attainment' (DES/WO 1988: 3.25).

Traditionally, only high-attaining pupils in secondary school had experienced a broad mathematics curriculum, while the lower attainers had merely learnt arithmetic. There had been a gradual movement to a broad curriculum for all, and the introduction of the National Curriculum has assured that it is the right of all pupils to continue to receive a balanced mathematics curriculum.

In primary schools, aspects of mathematics that were traditionally seen as the preserve of the secondary school have been moved down into the primary curriculum through the introduction of National Curriculum levels. Primary teachers are now faced with the teaching of algebra and probability, together with some areas of shape and data handling that are new to this phase of schooling. However, some aspects of the Algebra attainment target have always been taught in primary schools, although not under this heading. For example, level 1 Algebra requires pupils to distinguish odd and even numbers, an aspect of number work often taught but seldom regarded by primary teachers as algebra.

The content of the National Curriculum reflects much of the debate that has taken place over recent years about the introduction of 'modern mathematics' into the curriculum. The curriculum of the late 1960s and early 1970s was changed considerably with the introduction of sets, matrices, transformations, and vectors, and the removal of much of the traditional Euclidean geometry. At the same time, teaching for understanding rather than rote learning of skills was promoted. While much of this new content has been removed from the curriculum, the process of investigating within mathematics and problem-solving has gained credibility, and one attainment target in the latest version of the orders is devoted to the use and application of mathematics.

The curriculum has become streamlined, with more time devoted to ensuring that pupils' understanding of mathematics is enhanced in order that they may be more able to use and apply their skills to a variety of problems both familiar and unfamiliar.

The National Curriculum is not designed to be a strait-jacket, but is the minimum that ought to be covered. If and when the situation dictates, pupils can be given the opportunity to study related areas outside the bounds of the National Curriculum. This is particularly necessary when teachers are working with high-attaining pupils.

The first order for mathematics was published in 1989 and had fourteen attainment targets. This proved to be too unwieldy; it gave teachers too many individual statements of attainment to assess, and recording the progress of each pupil proved to be very time-consuming. The order was restructured in 1991 into five new attainment targets very similar in content to the previous order. The headings remain the same except for the attainment target 'Measure', which has been moved into 'Number' or 'Shape' as appropriate. The attainment targets should be considered together rather than as unrelated items. While the structure of individual attainment targets suggests a hierarchy of concepts with progression through the levels, there are also opportunities to teach across the attainment targets so that pupils see all aspects of mathematics as interrelated.

The new attainment targets are subdivided into strands as listed below (NCC 1991: introd. p. 5):

1. Using and Applying Mathematics	Applications
	Mathematical communication
	Reasoning, logic, and proof
2. Number	Knowledge and use of numbers
	Estimation and approximation
	Measures
3. Algebra	Patterns and relationships
	Formulae, equations, and inequalities
	Graphical representation
4. Shape and Space	Shape
	Location
	Movement
	Measures

5. Handling Data   Collecting and processing
                                Representing and interpreting
                                Probability

While the attainment targets specify what is to be assessed, the programmes of study specify a mathematics curriculum.

In the new Order most statements are broader than individual elements of the PoS. This means it is now possible to identify a key planning role for the PoS. Consequently the new layout shows PoS, SoA and examples alongside each other. The elements of the PoS are necessary in determining the scope of each SoA. (NCC 1991: introd. p. 4)

An example of this is AT2 level 4, which states:

1. Solve problems without the aid of a calculator, considering the reasonableness of the answer.
2. Demonstrate an understanding of the relationship between place values in whole numbers.
3. Use fractions, decimals, or percentages as appropriate to describe situations.
4. Solve number problems with the aid of a calculator, interpreting the display.
5. Make sensible estimates of a range of measures in relation to everyday objects.

In the previous order there were twelve statements of attainment targets for number at level 4. At level 4, AT2 (Number) had six statements, AT3 (Number) had three statements, and AT8 (Measures) had three statements. A closer examination of these reveals that some of the statements have been combined and there is some slight rewording to form the new statements.

The statutory elements are the attainment targets; this allows teachers to exercise their own professional judgement as to how they make use of the programmes of study and the examples that go alongside them. So, for example, a part of AT4, Shape and Space, level 5, looks like this:

Programme of study	Measuring and drawing angles to the nearest degree.
Statement of attainment	(a) Use accurate measurement and drawing in constructing 3D models.
Examples	Construct prisms; make a pyramid-shaped gift box of given dimensions.

Some statements have changed levels in the new order to take into account teachers' experience of working with the old order. Non-statutory guidance material has been produced which provides excellent guidelines on the implementation of the National Curriculum order.

The report of the working group acknowledged the contribution of computers in the world of work and indeed made an attempt to indicate how they might be used in some of the examples in the original order. The pace at which computer technology has moved forward, however, was not acknowledged in the new order. Many of the original examples are there in a similar form, but there is no guidance as to what impact computers have had on the mathematics curriculum at higher levels in particular. There are now sophisticated graphing packages available, symbolic manipulators which will solve a whole range of algebraic problems, as well as dynamic drawing packages for aspects of shape and space.

Northern Ireland

The National Curriculum for Northern Ireland is similar in structure to the original National Curriculum for England and Wales. There are thirteen attainment targets with ten levels:

- P_1, Processes in Mathematics, is similar in nature to maths AT_1 and states that 'pupils should develop mathematical processes through practical tasks, real-life problems and investigations within mathematics itself'.
- N_1, 2, and 3 are concerned with all aspects of number: N_1 covers number and number notation, N_2 covers number operations and methods for the use of appropriate methods of calculation, while N_3 covers estimation and approximation.
- A_1 is a number/algebra attainment target addressing patterns, relationships, sequences, and generality, while A_2 and A_3 are concerned with functions, formulae, and inequalities and the graphical representation of algebraic functions, respectively.
- M_1 is the measures attainment target and S_1 and S_2 cover aspects of shape and space including the properties of two and three dimensions; shapes, location, and transformation in space. Data-handling issues are covered in D_1 and D_2 and probability in D_3.

Assessment

The assessment of the mathematics curriculum has been the subject of much controversy and debate. Testing of 7-year-olds at the end of key stage 1 took place for the first time in 1991 and at key stage 3 in 1992. The debate has raged over the nature of those tests, how much weight is given to teacher assessment, as well as the publication of 'league tables'. It has been argued that some aspects of mathematics cannot easily be assessed through traditional pencil and paper methods, and unless teacher assessment of these aspects is given greater credibility then only the nationally tested aspects of the curriculum will be taught.

Key stage 1 SATs test a selection of attainment targets through a range of practical and pencil and paper tasks. The first tests in 1991 were a pilot but essentially the tests have stayed very much the same in format although there has been an increasing emphasis on AT2, Number.

Ring Game

Imagine you are playing a ring game.

How could you score 13 with 2 throws?

_____ and _____

What is the highest score you could get with 2 throws?

_____

At key stages 2 and 3 the SATs assess ATs 2–5. AT1 is assessed by teacher assessment. The SATs for key stage 2 were piloted in 1993 and for key stage 3 in 1992. Pupils are assessed by how well they perform at a particular level. There are four bands of tests and it is left to the teacher's discretion at which band each pupil is entered. There are three papers each of one hour's duration for the four bands. The bands are grouped for levels 1–4, 3–6, 5–8, and 7–10 respectively, thus allowing for a margin of error, so that a pupil who was considered to be no more than level 5 would be entered for band 3–6 and a pupil who was a good level 6 candidate would be entered for band 5–8.

(a) You cannot draw a right-angled triangle with edges 8cm, 12cm and 18cm.
Use Pythagoras' theorem to show why.
Show all your calculations.

2 marks
4/7c

(b) Is it possible to draw a triangle with the measurements shown in the diagram below?
Use sine, cosine or tangent to show why.
Show all your calculations.

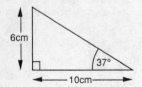

2 marks
4/8b

$$x^2 + y^2 = r^2 \quad \text{(Pythagoras' theorem)}$$

$$x = r\cos\theta \qquad y = r\sin\theta \qquad y = x\tan\theta$$

$$\cos\theta = \frac{x}{r} \qquad \sin\theta = \frac{y}{r} \qquad \tan\theta = \frac{y}{x}$$

Science

Introducing changes in the school curriculum is far from easy. All sorts of vested interests amongst teachers, parents, and the public at large can be threatened. Some research in the 1980s showed how the pupils themselves can prove resistant to innovation. In many ways this is a healthy reaction. The education system is susceptible to fads and fancies, and a degree of healthy scepticism is often warranted. It is, however, strange that only in the 1990s has the teaching of science become a priority issue in both primary and secondary schools. From the 1960s onwards scientists, science teachers, and industrialists have argued strongly for science curriculum reform. Even the Royal Society gave prestigious support to the need for change. In Chapter 2 the patchy, even non-existent provision in primary schools was commented on. At secondary level the divisions into physics, chemistry, and biology have meant that significant issues such as earth sciences or astronomy have been ignored. At the age of 14 some pupils dropped science completely, and others may have opted to continue the study of just one subject. Many boys chose physics and ignored biology. For girls it was the reverse. The National Curriculum plans for science aim to put an end to these inconsistencies. School science may continue to be taught by specialists, especially at secondary level, but every pupil is now entitled to a balanced science curriculum, covering all the major scientific disciplines.

The statutory orders in science describe four attainment targets for pupils. Each of these attainment targets is subdivided into strands of progression which describe how the main scientific ideas develop through the National Curriculum levels. In ATs 2–4 each strand helps to highlight aspects of science. AT1 is also described in terms of strands, but investigations must be holistic, that is, they must provide opportunities for pupils to demonstrate competence in at least two of the strands. Pupils must also be given opportunities to communicate their ideas and strategies in appropriate and effective ways.

There should be a parity between the level at which the investigation is being carried out in AT1 and the levels of knowledge and understanding in ATs 2–4. For example, an investigation pupils are carrying out at level 6 should relate to the knowledge and understanding at around levels 5 to 7 in ATs 2, 3, or 4.

AT1.	Scientific Investigation	(i)	Ask questions, predict, and hypothesize;
		(ii)	observe, measure, and manipulate variables;
		(iii)	interpret their results and evaluate scientific evidence.
AT2.	Life and Living Processes	(i)	Life-processes and the organization of living things;
		(ii)	variation and the mechanisms of inheritance and evolution;
		(iii)	populations and human influences within eco-systems;
		(iv)	energy-flows and cycles of matter within ecosystems.
AT3.	Materials and their Properties	(i)	The properties, classification, and structure of materials;
		(ii)	explanations of the properties of materials;
		(iii)	chemical changes;
		(iv)	the Earth and its atmosphere.
AT4.	Physical Processes	(i)	Electricity and magnetism;
		(ii)	energy resources and energy transfer;
		(iii)	forces and their effects;
		(iv)	light and sound;
		(v)	the Earth's place in the Universe.

This is called 'Double Science'.

There is a second, modified version of the National Curriculum in science, termed 'Single Science'. Pupils, in consultation with teachers and parents, can opt for either Double Science or Single Science in the final stage of secondary schooling at key stage 4.

Single Science is a more restricted programme that can be studied in less time. As a rule of thumb, Double Science assumes the study of science for 20 per cent of the school's weekly timetable, Single Science for 12.5 per cent.

'Single Science' contains the following attainment targets:

AT1.	Scientific Investigation	(i)	Ask questions, predict, and hypothesize;
		(ii)	observe, measure, and manipulate variables;
		(iii)	interpret their results and evaluate scientific evidence.
AT2.	Life and Living Processes	(i)	Life-processes and the organization of living things;
		(ii)	variation and the mechanisms of inheritance and evolution.
AT3.	Materials and their Properties	(i)	The properties, classification, and structure of materials;
		(ii)	explanations of the properties of materials.
AT4.	Physical Processes	(i)	Electricity and magnetism;
		(ii)	energy resources and energy transfer;
		(iii)	forces and their effects.

The list below shows how the attainment targets are planned in relation to key stages.

Key stage 1: supports ATs 1–4 (all strands); levels 1–3;
Key stage 2: supports ATs 1–4 (all strands); levels 2–5;
Key stage 3: supports ATs 1–4 (all strands); levels 3–7;
Key stage 4: Double Science: supports ATs 1–4 (all strands); levels 4–10.
Single Science: supports AT1 (strands i–iii), AT2 (strands i and ii), AT3 (strands i and ii), AT4 (strands i–iii); levels 4–10.

There has been considerable controversy about the Double Science/Single Science approach, with the majority of science education experts arguing that all key stage 4 children should experience the Double Science programme. This is an area where modifications may occur, though GCSE examining boards have begun publishing both Double Science and Single Science syllabuses in response to the statutory orders. Schools, and science teachers in particular, will be able to monitor these different approaches during implementation.

Examples of what can be expected of children in primary school at key stage 1 are set out below. Two examples are given for AT1, Scientific Investigation, and AT2, Life and Living Processes.

Attainment target 1: Scientific Investigation

Statements of attainment

Pupils should carry out investigations by which they:

Level 1:

  (a) observe familiar materials and events.

Level 2:

  (a) ask questions such as 'how . . . ?', 'why . . . ?', and 'what will happen if . . . ?', suggest ideas, and make predictions;
  (b) make a series of related observations;
  (c) use their observations to support conclusions, and compare what they have observed with what they expected.

Level 3:

  (a) suggest questions, ideas, and predictions, based on everyday experience, which can be tested;
  (b) observe closely and quantify by measuring using appropriate instruments;
  (c) recognize that their conclusions may not be valid unless a fair test has been carried out;
  (d) distinguish between a description of what they observed and a simple explanation of how and why it happened.

Attainment target 2: Life and Living Processes

Statements of attainment

Pupils should:

Level 1:

  (a) be able to name the main external parts of the human body and a flowering plant;
  (b) know that there is a wide variety of living things, which includes humans.

Level 2:

(a) know that plants and animals need certain conditions to sustain life;

(b) be able to sort familiar living things into broad groups according to easily observable features;

(c) know that different kinds of living things are found in different localities;

(d) know that some waste materials decay naturally but do so over different periods of time.

Level 3:

(a) know the basic life-processes common to humans and other animals;

(b) know that human activity may produce changes in the environment that can affect plants and animals;

(c) know that green plants need light to stay alive and healthy.

Higher-attaining secondary pupils in the same attainment targets will be expected to attempt the sort of work set out at levels 8, 9, and 10.

Attainment target 1: Scientific Investigation

Pupils should:

Level 8:

(a) use scientific knowledge, understanding, or theory to generate quantitative predictions and a strategy for the investigation;

(b) select and use measuring instruments which provide the degree of accuracy commensurate with the outcome they have predicted;

(c) justify each aspect of the investigation in terms of the contribution to the overall conclusion.

Level 9:

(a) use a scientific theory to make quantitative predictions and organize the collection of valid and reliable data;

(b) systematically use a range of investigatory techniques to judge the relative effect of the factors involved;

(c) analyse and interpret the data obtained, in terms of complex functions where appropriate, in a way which demonstrates an appreciation of the uncertainty of evidence and the tentative nature of conclusions.

Level 10:

(a) use scientific knowledge and an understanding of laws, theories, and models to develop hypotheses which seek to explain the behaviour of objects and events they have studied;

(b) collect data which are sufficiently valid and reliable to enable them to make a critical evaluation of the law, theory, or model;

(c) use and analyse the data obtained to evaluate the law, theory, or model in terms of the extent to which it can explain the observed behaviour.

Attainment target 2: Life and Living Processes

Pupils should:

Level 8:

(a) be able to describe how the internal environment in plants, animals, and the human embryo is maintained;

(b) know how genetic information is passed from cell to cell and from generation to generation by cell division;

(c) understand the principles of a monohybrid cross involving dominant and recessive alleles;

(d) understand that the impact of human activity on the Earth is related to the size of the population, economic factors, and industrial requirements;

(e) understand the role of microbes and other living organisms in the process of decay and in the cycling of nutrients.

Level 9:

(a) be able to explain the co-ordination in mammals of the body's activities through nervous and hormonal control;

(b) understand the different sources of genetic variation;

(c) understand the relationships between variation, natural selection, and reproductive success in organisms and the significance of these relationships for evolution;

(d) understand the basic scientific principles associated with a major change in the biosphere;

(e) understand how materials for growth and energy are trans-ferred through an ecosystem.

Level 10:

(a) understand how homeostatic and metabolic processes con-tribute to maintaining the internal environment of organ-isms;

(b) understand how DNA replicates and controls protein synthe-sis by means of a base code;

(c) understand the basic principles of genetic engineering, selec-tive breeding, and cloning, and how these give rise to social and ethical issues;

(d) understand how food production involves the management of ecosystems to improve the efficiency of energy transfer, and that such management imposes a duty of care.

There are numerous justifications for the teaching of science to all pupils. The expert group that came up with the recommenda-tions for the balanced programme provided an eloquent statement of advocacy.

The contribution of science in the school curriculum

Schools have an important role to play in helping children to under-stand the world they live in, and in preparing them for adult life and work. We are mindful of the value of our task in helping to equip these citizens of the next century with an education which should stand them in good stead in a world that will be very different from our own. We believe that science has an essential contribution to make in the following ways:

(1) Understanding scientific ideas

Scientists have developed a powerful body of knowledge about physi-cal and biological phenomena. Science education should provide opportunities for all pupils to develop an understanding of key con-cepts and enable them to be used in unfamiliar situations. To allow this to happen, pupils need to understand and explore their use in a range of contexts; the study of pure or formal science by itself can lead to ineffective learning by many pupils. Technological applications, per-sonal health or the environment can often provide contexts through which scientific concepts can be more effectively introduced and developed.

(2) Developing scientific methods of investigation

All pupils should be enabled to learn and to use scientific methods of investigation. They should have the opportunity to develop the skills of imaginative but disciplined enquiry which include systematic observation, making and testing hypotheses, designing and carrying out experiments competently and safely, drawing inferences from evidence, formulating and communicating conclusions in an appropriate form and applying them to new situations. Pupils should come to learn how to gain access to, and use selectively and appropriately, published scientific knowledge.

(3) Relating science to other areas of knowledge

Just as science cannot offer an adequate explanation of our world on its own, so science education needs to relate to other areas of the school curriculum. Pupils should be encouraged to recognise and value the contribution which science can make to other areas of learning, and the knowledge, skills and inspiration which scientists can derive from other activities.

(4) Understanding the contribution science makes to society

Pupils should be encouraged to study the practical applications of science and technology and the ways they are changing the nature of our society and our economy. They should be helped to explore some of the moral dilemmas that scientific discoveries and technological developments can cause. Science education should encourage all pupils to appreciate their responsibilities as members of society and give them the confidence to make a positive contribution to it.

(5) Recognizing the contribution science education makes to personal development

Productive learning needs the right conditions. Successful science and technology education requires pupils to combine interest and curiosity with a responsible attitude towards safety, and a respect for living organisms and the physical environment. It should help to develop other attitudes such as a willingness to accept uncertainty, to co-operate with others, to give honest reports, and to think critically. A study of science is an important dimension of health education, and pupils should become aware of its relevance to matters of personal and public health. Understanding and clarifying one's own thinking is often an essential part of learning. Throughout their science education, pupils should be encouraged to develop their powers of reasoning by reflecting on their own understanding, and by appreciating that learning may involve a change in the way they think about, explain and do things.

(6) Appreciating the nature of scientific knowledge

Pupils should further their understanding of science by exploring the social and historical contexts of scientific discoveries. Through this they can begin to appreciate the powerful but provisional nature of scientific explanation, and the process by which models are created, tested and modified in the light of evidence. Most important of all, they will be reminded of the excitement of discovery that has been the continual inspiration of all scientists.

Recent developments in our understanding of the way children learn have been incorporated into the programmes and advice for the teaching of science. For example, practical investigative approaches are given a prominent place through the first attainment target. Investigative abilities are seen to develop as the children mature and as they are brought into contact with new contexts and areas of knowledge. Skills of investigation and knowledge of the attainment targets are seen to develop alongside positive attitudes towards the subject. A lively and imaginative science programme can help children develop the following:

- curiosity;
- respect for evidence;
- willingness to tolerate uncertainty;
- critical reflection;
- perseverance;
- creativity and inventiveness;
- open-mindedness;
- sensitivity to the living and non-living environment;
- co-operation with others.

A parent who went to school in the 1950s, 1960s, or even 1970s would probably find that science is the subject in which there has been the most significant change. Experiments and investigations should now feature in most lessons. The situation where the teacher demonstrates an experiment which the pupils then try to copy exactly will be very rare. Experimentation is much more open-ended than it used to be.

The Council's non-statutory (not legally binding) guidance to teachers describes a primary school where the staff have planned the science curriculum around a chart (Fig. 7). Each class teacher chooses two segments from the chart each year. A record is kept to avoid repetition, and this is built into the school's record-keeping system. A teacher might plan a year's work in the following way

Autumn term	Fruits and seeds
	Moving toys
Spring term	Water
	Senses
Summer term	Light and colour
	Seaside

Part of the 'Moving toys' topic includes an investigation which looks at how windmills work. Following class discussion of a toy windmill, the children are divided into groups to make a model windmill. The guidance describes four different ways in which the teacher could organize the groups:

- *Approach A*: Discussion of task, and why tackle it. Take a sheet of paper cut to the right size with marking on it and instructions on what to do with it—cut, fold, stick, make hole, attach, etc. Explore how to make it rotate (near heater, running in the playground holding up high in windiest spot). Oral communication, picture painting.

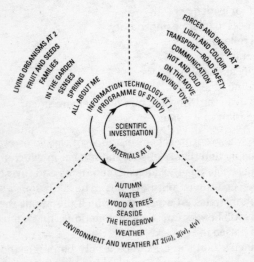

Fig. 7 Map of a Scheme of Work

- *Approach B*: After group discussion of task and the variety of papers which could be used, decide which might be used to make a paper windmill similar to the real one; use a template to cut and then make (using example). Try to rotate in different situations, compare findings with others, consider what makes them move differently. Oral communication, simple tick chart.

- *Approach C*: The group discuss and consider how they might make a paper windmill (no example given), with stimulus of range of materials, including paper cups for example, with opportunity then to try out own ideas, make, modify, remake, gather the resulting models, test in similar ways and compare. Collate and record results in appropriate ways.

- *Approach D*: Making a windmill according to an agreed format, after initial stage of exploration. Identification of variables that may affect the efficiency of the windmill, e.g. size of paper, type of material, number of vanes, means of attaching to rod, etc. Groups to select and test one variable, combine results at end. Display results graphically, interpret findings, make a generalized statement, choose the best material, number of vanes, etc., to make a 'super windmill'.

At the primary level, the teacher will also be thinking about simultaneous development towards attainment targets in English and mathematics. There are clearly important links with technology as well.

At the secondary level, science will almost always be taught as a separate subject with specialist laboratories available. AT12, Scientific Investigation, will be central to the curriculum, although most lessons and activities will incorporate one or more additional attainment targets.

The advice given to teachers by the National Curriculum Council offers a number of examples of how this can be achieved. 'Pupils could be set a task on house insulation. This would involve them in looking at their own house, and testing materials to see which provides the best insulation. At the end of the project they could write a report to their parents on how to economise on energy!' Pupils would be developing the relevant competences at level 6 of AT1. For example, pupils should carry out investigations in which they:

Level 6:

    (*a*) use scientific knowledge and understanding of theory to predict relationships between continuous variables;

    (*b*) consider the range of factors involved, identify the key variables and those to be controlled and/or taken account of, and make qualitative or quantitative observations involving fine discrimination.

As an example, pupils might use their knowledge of the properties of materials in heat insulation to predict a relationship between the fall of temperature of hot water in a vessel against time for a particular insulating material. They should be able to identify the two continuous variables—time and temperature—and identify those variables to be controlled such as the thickness of the insulating material, the volume of hot water in the vessel, and the ambient temperature.

They would also be covering parts of AT4, strand ii, across levels 5, 6, and 7.

Attainment target 4: Physical Processes

Pupils should:

Level 5:

    (*b*) understand that energy is transferred in any process and recognize transfers in a range of devices;

    (*c*) understand the difference between renewable and non-renewable energy resources and the need for fuel economy.

Level 6:

    (*b*) understand that energy is conserved;

    (*c*) understand that the Sun is ultimately the major energy source for the Earth.

Level 7:

    (*b*) understand how energy is transferred through conduction, convection, and radiation;

    (*c*) be able to evaluate methods of reducing wasteful transfers of energy by using a definition of energy efficiency.

A further example is an investigation to find out how light and temperature affect the growth rate of cress. The pupils here could be working at level 7 of AT1. At this level they are expected to manipulate independent variables and to use their results to draw conclusions which state the relative effects of the independent variables and explain the limitations of the evidence they obtain. They will be looking at how many different temperatures and how many different intensities of light are sufficient to give an answer to the problem. AT2 will be covered in this topic.

A final example, at a more advanced level, is in the area of the properties, classification, and structure of materials and of chemical changes. Pupils could look at the alternative merits of different forms of protection against corrosion (for example, paints, electrolytic coatings, galvanizing). The sort of skills that could be developed at levels 8, 9, and 10 are given on pp. oo–o (AT1, Scientific Investigation). The extract below from AT3 shows the knowledge targets that would be included in the teacher's plans.

Attainment target 3: Materials and their Properties

Pupils should:

Level 8:

  (*a*) know the major characteristics of metals and non-metals as reflected in the properties of a range of compounds;
  (*f*) be able to use symbolic equations to describe and explain a range of reactions including ionic interactions and those occurring in electrolytic cells.

Level 9:

  (*a*) understand how the properties of elements depend on their electronic structure and their position in the periodic table;
  (*c*) be able to interpret chemical equations quantitatively;
  (*d*) be able to use scientific information from a range of sources to evaluate the social, economic, health and safety, and environmental factors associated with a major manufacturing process.

Level 10:

  (*a*) be able to use data on the properties of different materials in order to make evaluative judgements about their uses;
  (*d*) be able to interpret electrolytic processes quantitatively.

End of key stage tests

One example of a key stage 1 test for assessment purposes is given below:

Which of these will decay?

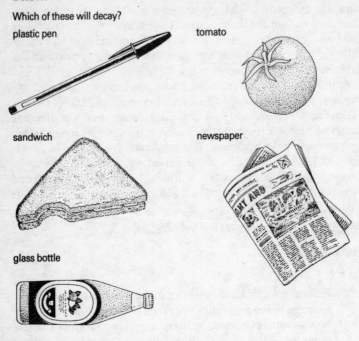

plastic pen

tomato

sandwich

newspaper

glass bottle

The things I have chosen will all take the same time to decay.

YES   NO

Two examples of end of key stage 3 tests are illustrated below. The examples differ in the levels at which pupils taking the tests are expected to attain. Thus the question relating to Earth's place in the Universe from AT4 reflects levels of knowledge and understanding between levels 3 and 6. For the example on inheritance, pupils are expected to demonstrate levels of knowledge and understanding between levels 5 and 7.

The drawings show the Moon on different nights during the month of June.

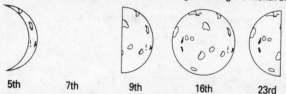

5th   7th   9th   16th   23rd   26th

(a)   Draw what the Moon looks like on June 7th.

1 mark

(b)   Draw what the Moon looks like on June 26th.

1 mark

The drawing below shows the position of the Sun in the sky at midday on 21st March.

the Sun at midday

horizon

On the drawing above, draw circles to show the position of the Sun:

(c)   at midday on 21st December. Label it D.

1 mark

(d)   at midday on 21st June. Label it J.

1 mark

(e)   Sunrise is 8.30 am on 21st December. Will sunrise on the 21st June be earlier, later, or at the same time?

_____

1 mark

Two different varieties of tomato plant *A* and *B* were bred together. This produced a new variety.

The diagrams show all **three** varieties of tomato plant bearing ripe fruit.

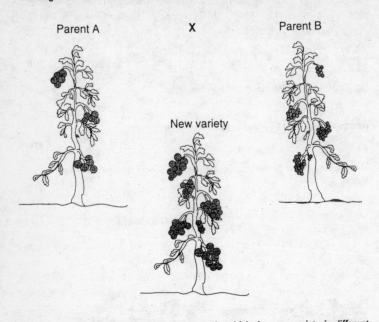

Parent A   X   Parent B

New variety

(a) Give **two** ways, shown in the diagrams, in which the new variety is different from the parent varieties.

2 marks

1. _____

_____

2. _____

_____

(b) Suggest **one** other characteristic of the tomatoes from the new variety which might be different from the tomatoes of either parent.

1 mark

_____

(c) Researchers at a research farm wish to try and improve the new variety further. They start with the tomato seeds from the new variety.

Describe steps they should take in this new selective breeding experiment.

2 marks

_____

_____

Northern Ireland

The Northern Ireland science curriculum has a similar structure to that of England and Wales, but there are some differences in content. There are five attainment targets in the Northern Ireland curriculum. These are:

AT1. Exploring and Investigating in Science;
AT2. Living Things;
AT3. Materials;
AT4. Forces and Energy;
AT5. Environment.

The Single Science alternative programme of study for key stage 4 consists of the first four attainment targets only. It should be noted, however, that knowledge and understanding of the topic Environment appears within these four attainment targets. Single Science is a subset of the Double Award with slight amendments to ensure it is a coherent programme of study.

Information technology appears in the statements of attainment in AT1. For example, AT1/7/c: pupils should be able to 'use IT devices to monitor and control experiments'. In the Northern Ireland curriculum IT is a cross-curricular theme. Cross-curricular themes are a statutory part of the Northern Ireland curriculum and appear within the programmes of study and statements of attainment.

It should be noted that this is the situation as of October 1993. There are current proposals to reduce the number of attainment targets to four, with an Environment strand being included within ATs 2, 3, and 4 instead of a separate Environment attainment target. Strands have been identified to show progression through each attainment target and the existing statements of attainment have been revised. In particular the statements of attainment at the higher levels of AT1 have been modified.

6 The Foundation Subjects: Technology, History, Geography, Modern Languages, Art, Music, Physical Education

The foundation subjects are all undergoing review in 1994 and revised statutory orders will take effect from September 1995. The descriptions below describe the background to the way the subject is taught today within the existing national curriculum framework.

Technology

The introduction of technology into the primary and secondary curriculum is one of the major innovations of the National Curriculum. For some time, a growing body of opinion had been arguing for technology to be given far greater importance at all levels of schooling. This was acknowledged in the first consultation document on the National Curriculum, and the technology working party was the first to be set up after the core foundation subject groups. The final report it produced was one of the least controversial, perhaps in part because so few people had had direct experience of the subject in their own school-days. The National Curriculum Council, in the foreword of the document that made the final recommendations to the Secretary of State, underlined why every child should study technology:

Technology is the one subject in the National Curriculum that is directly concerned with generating ideas, making and doing. In emphasising the importance of practical capability, and providing opportunities for pupils to develop their powers to innovate, to make decisions, to create new solutions, it can play a unique role. Central to this role is the task of providing balance in a curriculum based on academic subjects—a balance in which the creative and practical capabilities of pupils can be fully developed and inter-related. The subject has a crucial part to play in helping pupils to develop these important personal qualities and competencies.

Whilst the contribution of technology to the personal development of individuals is very important, of equal importance is its role in helping pupils to respond to the employment needs of business and industry. Pupils will become aware of technological development, and the way in which technology is changing the workplace and influencing lifestyles. They will learn that technological change cannot be reversed, and will understand its enormous power. Knowledge of technology enables citizens to be prepared to meet the needs of the 21st century and to cope with a rapidly changing society.

This dual justification, for personal development and in developing an awareness of the needs of business and industry, is reflected in the programmes of study and the attainment targets. There are five attainment targets. The first four are grouped together as one profile component (Design and Technology Capability) for reporting to parents.

AT1. Identifying Needs and Opportunities: pupils should be able to identify and state clearly needs and opportunities for design and technological activities through investigation of the contexts of home, school, recreation, community, business, and industry.

AT2. Generating a Design: pupils should be able to generate a design specification, explore ideas to produce a design proposal, and develop it into a realistic, appropriate, and achievable design.

AT3. Planning and Making: pupils should be able to make artefacts, systems, and environments, preparing and working to a plan and identifying, managing, and using appropriate resources, including knowledge and processes.

AT4. Evaluating: pupils should be able to develop, communicate, and act upon an evaluation of the processes, products, and effects of their design and technological activities and of those of others, including those from other times and cultures.

The fifth attainment target corresponds to the second profile component (Information Technology Capability):

AT5. Information Technology Capability: pupils should be able to use information technology to:

- communicate and handle information;
- design, develop, explore, and evaluate models of real or imaginary situations;
- measure and control physical variables and movement.

They should be able to make informed judgements about the application and importance of information technology and its effect on the quality of life.

Within the technology attainment targets, information technology capability is given a specific place (AT5). As many National Curriculum documents make clear, information technology (IT) plays a part in the teaching of most subjects, and IT should not be regarded as another subject. AT5 is placed within technology for the purpose of reporting, but IT capability is achieved across a range of different subjects, design and technology being one context amongst many. The list below shows how the attainment targets are planned to relate to key stages 1–3:

Key stage 1: ATs 1–5; levels 1–3
Key stage 2: ATs 1–5; levels 2–5
Key stage 3: ATs 1–5; levels 3–7

The statutory order in technology is set out in a different way from those in the core foundation subjects. The attainment targets are less about the content of the subject and more about the way of doing it. Educationalists talk about the *process* of generating ideas, making, and doing. A review of the order in 1992 drew attention to the difficulties teachers were having in working with AT1 (Identifying Needs and Opportunities) and AT4 (Evaluating), and the National Curriculum Council considered that, because of this, pupils were spending too little time on practical designing and making. The Council recommended that pupils' work should be concentrated on ATs 2 and 3, with pupils evaluating what they have done as and when appropriate. Examples of what can be expected of children in the primary school from ATs 2 and 3 are set out below.

Pupils should be able to generate a design specification, explore ideas to produce a design proposal, and develop it into a realistic, appropriate, and achievable design.

Level	Statements of attainment	Examples
	Pupils should be able to:	
1	Express their ideas about what they might do to meet an identified need or opportunity.	Draw pictures showing different ways of scaring birds in a field of crops.
2	Use talk, pictures, drawings, models, to develop their design proposals, giving simple reasons why they have chosen to make their design.	Explain why they have chosen to make bird-scarers. Draw a picture showing how they will make a scarecrow and say how it will scare away the birds from crops.
3	Make a design proposal by selecting from their ideas and giving reasons for their choices.	Explain why they have chosen certain features of their different designs for a desk-tidy to use in their design proposal.
	Apply knowledge and skills to select ideas for different parts of their design.	Choose from a range of designs and materials produced by their class for the front cover and contents of a class book on pets.
	Draw from information about materials, people, markets, and processes and from other times and cultures to help in developing their ideas.	Gather information on different types of ethnic food and peoples' preferences when planning a party.
	Use models including annotated drawings and three-dimensional working models to develop their designs.	Use a model, drawing, or an existing example, to try out different ideas for the detail of a bird-scarer.
	Record how they have explored different ideas about a design and technological proposal to see how realistic it might be.	Record different designs for bird-scarers, a rattle, a kite.

Pupils should be able to make artefacts, systems, and environments, preparing and working to a plan and identifying, managing and using appropriate resources, including knowledge and processes.

Level	Statements of attainment	Examples
	Pupils should be able to:	
1	Use a variety of materials and equipment to make simple things.	Use scissors, paper, and paint to make a decorative protection for a display table.

Table continued

Level	Statements of attainment	Examples
2	Describe to others how they are going about their work.	Describe their actions to their group or to a visitor.
	Use knowledge of the working characteristics of materials and components, including construction kits, in making artefacts, systems, or environments.	When building a model roundabout, use sandpaper to smooth wood, allow enough time for the paint to dry.
	Show that they can use simple hand-tools, materials, and components.	Use tools for cutting and shaping clay to make a model.
3	Consider constraints of time and availability of resources in planning and making.	
	Choose resources for making by using their knowledge of the characteristics of materials and components.	Where glue is used in making a mobile, choose a type appropriate to the materials used.
	Use a range of hand-tools and equipment, appropriate to the materials and components, with some regard for accuracy and quality.	Choose an appropriate tool to drill, cut, smooth, and join different materials such as wood, clay, paper, card, fabric, polystyrene, to make a boat.
	Improvise within the limits of materials, resources, and skills when faced with unforeseen difficulties.	When a glue will not stick a model together, recognize that alternative methods might work instead, e.g. another glue, staples, Sellotape.

High-attaining secondary pupils, in the same attainment targets, will be expected to attempt the work set out at levels 8, 9, 10.

Level	Statements of attainment	Examples
8	Record and present, using a range of methods and media, the progress of their ideas; detail and refine their design proposal and incorporate modifications; use computer-aided design, image-generation, and desk-top publishing techniques, where appropriate, to explore, detail, and refine their ideas.	Present interim ideas for a school magazine, using mock-ups and scale drawings, and use audience feedback to refine the design using computer-supported editing techniques.

Level	Statements of attainment	Examples
	Plan their activities to take into account multiple constraints which may at times be conflicting.	Make a plan for a piece of jewellery within a fixed budget. Match the size and complexity of the piece with the cost of the material and the time required to make it.
	Show a willingness, subject to safety considerations, to experiment and take risks recognizing the implications of decisions taken in designing.	Produce a design proposal for an experimental new food product. Explore ideas involving novel uses of common materials (cf. concrete in boatbuilding).
9	Develop ideas by drawing on information and understanding from a broad knowledge of sources, and showing judgement about the detail required.	Bringing together the best parts of different ideas after further research. How could the design be improved? What problems are still likely to exist and how could the design be changed to overcome these? Know when they have enough information of sufficient accuracy for the next stage of development of their design proposal.
	Refine their design to achieve an optimum practicable outcome, demonstrating originality and understanding of constraints in the justification of their design.	Develop a series of linked spreadsheets to be used by a builder to calculate the cost of building home extensions.
10	Provide a substantiated account of the full range of ideas they have explored and the strategies used, showing: 1. how they explored ideas used in existing artefacts, systems, or environments, and how they used them to develop their own ideas; 2. evidence that they have: (a) identified ways of improving and refining their proposals; (b) predicted with accuracy the	Through a presentation and exhibition, which includes a comprehensive folio of drawings, sketches, models, technical drawing, and other techniques, show evidence of thorough investigation of existing artefacts, systems, and environments, and how and why they incorporated some features of these and rejected others. It will also contain evidence of thorough research of needs and opportunities, original ideas, and a justification of all decisions taken

Table continued

Level	Statements of attainment	Examples
	outcomes of possible improvement; (c) resolved conflicting demands; (d) included their decisions in a coherent specification, and using an appropriate range of media and methods.	in refining their proposal, including fitness for purpose, experiments, tests, and trials.

Note: Pupils unable to communicate by speech, writing, or drawing may use other means, including the use of technology or symbols as alternatives.

Level	Statements of attainment	Examples
8	Review how to make best use of materials, procedures, tools, and equipment.	Experiment with alternative techniques in order to simplify or improve the methods of realisation of a design.
	Show evidence of knowledge of making processes and devise and implement procedures for quality assurance.	Develop quality assurance features within the planned production at key points, for example in silk screen printing.
	Identify and incorporate modifications during making.	Solve the problem of a blind spot on an infra-red detector by modifying positions of a sensor, introducing another type of sensor, or increasing sensitivity.
9	Make judgements about the quality and usefulness of sources of advice and information consulted during planning and making.	
	Demonstrate how they have overcome constraints encountered in planning and making to achieve a quality product.	
	Use knowledge of specialist conventions to assist making, to introduce improvements, and to explain what they are doing.	Produce a report using models, illustrations, text, and plans.

Level	Statements of attainment	Examples
10	Use a range of techniques, processes, and resources with confidence, safety, and creativity to achieve high-quality work.	Use a combination of computer-aided design and other high-quality graphic techniques to produce a house style and image for a new company.
	Review the design proposal during planning and making, and show resourcefulness and adaptability in modifying the design in the light of constraints, to make a high quality product.	

Note: Pupils unable to communicate by speech, writing, or drawing may use other means, including the use of technology or symbols as alternatives.

The prime rationale for technology is the process approach, because it can extend over so many different subjects and contexts. Established subjects such as craft, design, and technology (CDT), business studies, home economics, and computer studies are all incorporated into this approach to technology. Other subjects, aspects of art and science for example, could also be included. A second difference in the statutory orders is that the programmes of study relate generally to the key stages for each profile component, rather than to each attainment target. This is to emphasize an integrated approach to the way the subject is taught.

The general introduction to the programmes of study suggests that in their designing and making pupils should include different products such as:

- artefacts (objects made by people);
- systems (sets of objects or activities which together perform a task); and
- environments (surroundings made, or developed, by people).

These are not mutually exclusive. For example, a puppet could be regarded as an artefact with a particular finish and appearance, or as a system if the emphasis is on the mechanism for articulation. A greenhouse could be considered as an artefact (in relation to a shed), a system (in relation to temperature stability), or an environment for plants. What is intended is that over each key stage pupils should consider a range of products. Similarly, they should work with a range of materials (textiles, graphic media, construction materials, and food) and a range of contexts (home, school, recreation, community, and business and industry), although they do not have to give equal time to each aspect.

The programmes of study are based around four key themes:

1. Developing and Using Artefacts, Systems, and Environments;
2. Working with Materials;
3. Developing and Communicating Ideas;
4. Satisfying Needs and Addressing Opportunities.

In July 1993 it was proposed that teachers should give priority to the parts of the programme of study specifically concerned with designing and making: Developing and Using Artefacts, Systems, and Environments, and Working with Materials. To give an idea of what this means, an extract from the programme of study at key stage 1 is set out below.

Programme of study	Examples
Developing and Using Artefacts, Systems, and Environments	
Pupils should be taught to:	
Know that a system is made of related parts which are combined for a purpose.	A bicycle; a house.
Identify the jobs done by parts of a system.	A bicycle chain; a kitchen.
Give a sequence of instructions to produce a desired result.	Prepare a shopping-list in order of shops to be visited.
Recognize, and make models of, simple structures around them.	Making model buildings from simple construction kits.
Use sources of energy to make things move.	Stretched elastic bands to turn a propeller on a model plane; battery to make a toy move; moving things manually.
Identify what should be done and ways in which work should be organized.	Stamping a pattern on a fabric.
Working with Materials	
Pupils should be taught to:	
Explore and use a variety of materials	Use a variety of materials such as

Programme of study	Examples
to design and make things.	cotton-reels or building-blocks to make a tower; making a collage.
Recognize that materials are processed in order to change or control their properties.	Yeast dough to bread; clay to pot.
Recognize that many materials are available and have different characteristics which make them appropriate for different tasks.	Fabric, paper, card, clay, paint, wood; clay for making a beaker; newspaper for covering the table when painting.
Join materials and components in simple ways.	Gluing card, sewing on buttons.
Use materials and equipment safely.	

At the secondary level the programmes of study have a core of requirements for each key stage and additional requirements for pupils working to specific levels. As for key stages 1 and 2, priority is given to the aspects of the programme concerned with designing and making. Below are sections from key stage 3 relating to the extra sections in Developing and Using Artefacts, Systems, and Environments for those pupils working towards level 7, and Working with Materials for those pupils working towards levels 6 and 7. Following these are the additional requirements in Developing and Communicating Ideas and Satisfying Needs and Opportunities for those key stage 4 pupils working towards level 8.

Programme of study	Examples
Developing and Using Artefacts, Systems, and Environments	
Pupils should be taught to:	
Know that energy can be a significant cost in manufacture and in the use of a product or system.	
Recognize that people are an important resource and need to be trained, organized, and motivated.	Sharing responsibilities when making a stage set.
Design and make structures to take stationary and moving load.	A bridge to carry a model train.

Table continued

Programme of study	Examples
Recognize how the efficiency of a mechanism can be improved when designing a product.	Designing a buggy, study the effects of the design and the use of different materials on the distance the buggy travels.
Design mechanical systems to produce a desired output from a given input.	
Estimate the time taken, and the resources required, to complete each task and its components.	Arranging an event to sell products made in school.

Working with Materials

Pupils should be taught to:

Programme of study	Examples
Use a variety of material-processing equipment to develop craft skills involved in shaping, forming, joining, assembling, and rearranging.	Achieving a good fit, and attractive presentation.
Select and use appropriate methods of assembling a range of materials.	Choosing the appropriate stitch when sewing by hand or machine; soldering electronic components; gluing and pinning wood.
Recognize the purpose of pieces of equipment, to understand their handling characteristics, and the basic principles upon which they work.	How different saws cut wood.
Use computer-based systems as tools for designing and making.	Graphic programs with libraries of shapes and symbols, computer-controlled knitting-machines; printed circuit boards.
Recognize that products must be electrically and mechanically safe.	

Developing and Communicating Ideas

Pupils should be taught to:

Programme of study	Examples
Present their proposals to an audience, using a range of methods and media.	
Use computer-aided design, image generation, and desk-top publishing to develop and communicate their ideas.	Planning the detailed layout of a kitchen or recreation park; developing proposals for a company logo and letterhead.

Programme of study	Examples
Use symbols and conventions that have a meaning for an international audience	Designing working instructions, signposts for an airport; warning signs; using electronic symbols in printed circuit design.
Collate, sort, analyse, interpret, and present information in a logical and coherent way.	Justifying the choice of a site for a factory.
Recognize the place of experimentation and know that a new solution may be devised which has little basis in existing solutions.	Linear induction motor; hovercraft.

Satisfying Needs and Addressing Opportunities

Pupils should be taught to:

Review the ways in which market research can be used to evaluate user requirements and market potential.	Investigating the siting of a new supermarket; design of a graphics pen or drawing-board.
Understand that external influences (legal, environmental, social, health, safety) have effects on business activity.	Considering the restrictions imposed by the Data Protection Act or the need for green belts around towns.
Recognize the needs of individuals and groups from different backgrounds, when designing for their needs.	The need for different food, clothing, or shelter on the grounds of health, religion, or culture.
Recognize how economics affects design and technological activities and to work to a budget.	Designing to a fixed budget; making aids for the elderly.
Recognize the importance of the views of users and others affected by design proposals, and take them into account in taking design decisions.	High-rise and low-rise buildings; hypermarkets on the outskirts of towns; furniture design.
Distinguish between objective and subjective criteria when evaluating.	

Some of the titles and phrases have a ring of unfamiliarity about them. 'Addressing Opportunities' or 'Developing and Using Environments', for example, have only just come into the terminology of professional educationists, let alone the lay public.

Technology, however, is a new subject, and the way it is formulated for the National Curriculum is radically different from the myriad of versions of it that existed previously. A new subject needs new terms if it is to be meaningfully accurate across the variety of schools in England and Wales.

Most people are aware of the way this sort of change has affected information technology. Terminology that a few decades ago, if it existed at all, would have been familiar to only a few specialist scientists, now features in dozens of magazines that can be found in newsagents everywhere. The statutory orders describing the programmes of study for information technology also open with a number of general statements.

In each key stage pupils should develop information technology capabilities through a range of curriculum activities which will:

- develop confidence and satisfaction in the use of information technology;
- broaden pupils' understanding of the effects of the use of information technology;
- encourage the flexibility needed to take advantage of future developments in information technology;
- encourage the development of perseverance;
- enable pupils to take greater responsibility for their own learning, and provide opportunities for them to decide when it is appropriate to use information technology in their work.

A detailed specification for the different key stages then follows. Given the widespread interest in information technology and its relationship to other subjects, both the programme of study and the attainment targets in this area are given here in full. These illustrate the sort of development and progression the National Curriculum aims to promote across the whole age range.

Programme of study for key stage 1 (levels 1–3 (ages 5–7))

Pupils should be taught:

- that control is integral in many everyday products, such as cookers, cars, telephones;
- that information technology can be used to help plan and organize ideas in written and graphical form;

- how to give instructions to electronic devices, such as programmable toys and computers;
- how to store, select, and analyse information using software, for example, using a simple database package;
- that information technology can be used for tasks which can often also be accomplished by other means.

In addition, pupils working towards level 1 should be taught to:

- know that information can be held in a variety of forms, for example, words, numbers, pictures, sounds;
- know that it is not always necessary to use the computer keyboard in order to produce information, for example, by using an overlay keyboard to select musical phrases; by using a two-position switch to select from a menu;
- control everyday items, such as central-heating thermostats, and televisions, and describe the effects of their actions.

Pupils working towards level 2 should be taught to :

- know that IT can be used to store, modify, and retrieve information in words, pictures, and sounds;
- organize and present ideas using IT; for example, using a simple word-processor package.

Pupils working towards level 3 should be taught to:

- use software packages confidently and well;
- locate information stored in a database; retrieve information and add to it; check the accuracy of entries.

Programme of study for key stage 3 (levels 3–7 (ages 11–14))

Pupils should be taught to:

- integrate more than one form of information, for example, words and pictures; symbols; pictures and sound, into a single presentation or report for a particular audience;
- use desk-top publishing to write about population growth, illustrating with graphs and charts; develop a sequence of screens of information to introduce visitors to the school, co-ordinated with a spoken commentary on a tape-recorder;

- work together to prepare and present information using information technology;
- use information technology to work more effectively;
- (for example) use a word-processor for developing ideas for an essay; use a graphics program to investigate colour combinations for a design (instead of producing a series of design examples by hand);
- know that each software item has its own strengths and weaknesses, and that the selection of software involves consideration of the facilities offered, ease and simplicity of use, availability, and cost;
- select software for a task or application;
- (for example) choose between a word-processing or desk-top publishing package to produce a book for young readers; choose between a database or spreadsheet program to store data about the additives contained in popular foods;
- know that the use of information technology does not always provide an appropriate solution to a need, and that the effectiveness, appropriateness, and cost of alternative solutions must be considered;
- (for example) compare books, directories, and databases as means of storing and presenting information;
- know that information technology is used to monitor physical events and conditions, and to process, present, and respond to collected data, for example, monitor the dampness of the soil around houseplants, with a view to developing a self-watering system;
- review and discuss their use of information technology applications and to consider related applications in the outside world, and their impact on daily life, for example, compare the setting-up and running of a school viewdata system with that of a travel agent.

In addition, for pupils working towards level 3, teachers should refer to relevant material for key stage 1, and, for pupils working towards levels 4 and 5, teachers should refer to key stage 2.

Pupils working towards level 6 should be taught to:

- identify clearly the requirements, and make correct use of information technology equipment, software, and techniques, in making presentations and reports:

- (for example) combine text and images in different ways for a newspaper report and a poster; compose and play music to a class;
- modify the data and rules of a computer model;
- (for example) examine the development of a simulated colony of pond algae by varying the rules of reproduction.

Pupils working towards level 7 should be taught to:

- know that outcomes are affected by incorrect data, inappropriate procedures, limitations in the methods of data capture and the techniques of enquiry used to retrieve information; for example, compare the quality and quantity of data obtained by direct recording such as local weather statistics and remote recording by satellite monitoring;
- translate an enquiry expressed in ordinary language into forms required by information retrieval systems;
- use search methods to obtain accurate and relevant information from a database; for example, use a database where knowledge of Boolean logic will improve the efficiency of the enquiry;
- design a computer model for a specific purpose.

Pupils working towards level 8 should be taught to:

- define the information required, the purposes for which it is needed, and how it will be analysed; and to take these into account in designing ways of collecting and organizing the information when creating a database; for example, create a database to enable a paint manufacturer to identify customers' preferences for colour and type of paint;
- use information-handling software to capture, store, retrieve, analyse, and present information;
- know that the mathematical basis of a computer representation of a situation determines how accurately the model reflects reality; for example, a program to trace the trajectory of a tennis ball; a spreadsheet to anticipate trends in predator/prey populations;
- analyse a situation, and then design, implement, assess, and refine a complex model to represent it.

Pupils working towards level 10 should be taught to:

- analyse systems to be modelled using information technology, make choices in designing, implementing, and testing them, and justify the methods they have used.

Attainment target 5: Information Technology Capability

Level	Statements of attainment	Examples
	Pupils should be able to:	
1	Work with a computer.	Use an overlay keyboard to select items on a computer screen.
	Talk about ways in which equipment, such as toys and domestic appliances, responds to signals or commands.	Press a button to ring a door-bell; turn a knob to adjust the volume of a tape-recorder; observe the automatic switch on an electric kettle.
2	Use computer-generated pictures, symbols, words, or phrases to communicate meaning.	Select furniture for a house displayed on the computer screen, using an overlay keyboard; construct a simple story as a sequence of words, pictures, or sounds, using an overlay keyboard or mouse.
	Use information technology for the storage and retrieval of information.	Write about 'today's weather' using a word-processor so that the writing can be retrieved later.
3	Use information technology to make, amend, and present information.	Use a word-processor to draft a class diary; use information technology, with voices or conventional instruments, to make music and replay it.
	Give a sequence of direct instructions to control movement.	Give instructions to another pupil playing the part of a robot; control the movement of a screen turtle, using turtle graphics.
	Collect information and enter it in a database (whose structure may have been prepared in advance), and to select and retrieve information from the database.	Enter data recording the birds using the school bird-table, check the data, and retrieve it to compare the numbers and types of birds on different days.

Level	Statements of attainment	Examples
	Describe their use of information technology and compare it with other methods.	Write about the differences between using a programmable toy and giving instructions to another pupil; identify the differences between using pencil and paper and using information technology for handling information.
4	Use information technology to retrieve, develop, organize, and present work.	Produce a class newsletter or a set of information screens to give parents information about the school.
	Develop a set of commands to control the movement of a screen image or robot; understand that a computer program or procedure is a set of instructions to be followed in a predetermined sequence.	Drive a robot round on an obstacle course or maze; use turtle graphics to draw a house.
	Amend and add to information in an existing database, to check its plausibility and interrogate it.	Store personal information (such as name, height, weight, age, sex, shoe size, hair colour, eye colour), check it is correctly stored, and find the names of girls and boys with particular characteristics.
	Use a computer model to detect patterns and relationships, and how the rules governing the model work.	Use a program which simulates a trawler looking for fish, or an adventure program with a clearly defined objective.
	Review their experience of information technology and consider applications in everyday life.	Investigate overlay keyboards used in fast-food shops.
5	Use information technology to present information in different forms for specific purposes.	Edit a newspaper for parents; work together to produce a book for younger pupils.
	Understand that a computer can control devices by a series of commands, and appreciate the need for precision in framing commands.	Investigate control systems such as automatic doors and alarm systems; make a set of computer-controlled traffic lights.

Table continued

Level	Statements of attainment	Examples
	Use a software package to create a computer database so that data can be captured, stored, and retrieved.	Use information from a survey of prices of goods in local shops and markets.
	Use information technology to explore patterns and relationships, and to form and test simple hypotheses.	Using a simulation, explore how the populations of predator and prey species fluctuate, and suggest when a predator is most active.
	Understand that personal information may be held on computer, which is of interest to themselves and their families.	Collect correspondence received by their families which has been addressed using computer databases, and discuss data needed to produce it.
6	Use information technology to combine and organize different forms of information for a presentation to an audience.	Produce a report which involves use of different fonts and letter sizes, and illustrations.
	Understand that devices can be made to respond to data from sensors.	Use a computer to draw a graph of the temperature of a liquid as it cools; write a procedure, using a software package to provide a warning sound if a light-beam is interrupted.
	Identify advantages and limitations of data-handling programs and graphics programs, and recognize when these offer solutions to a problem of data handling.	Use a desk-top publishing program to integrate text and images in the report of a scientific experiment; choose a data-handling program for processing the results of sports day.
	Investigate and assess the consequences of varying the data or the rules within a simple computer model.	Define or change the way information is grouped into columns in a spreadsheet showing the nutritional values of types of meals; modify a turtle graphics procedure or its parameters to draw a variety of shapes and transform them.

Level	Statements of attainment	Examples
7	Select software and use it to produce reports which combine different forms of information to fulfil specific purposes for a variety of audiences.	Produce a presentation suited to a specific audience, combining graphics and text.
	Design, use, and construct a computer model of a situation or process, and construct computer procedures involving variables.	Model the queue of people waiting at a supermarket check-out and vary the service time, number of customers, and number of check-outs.
	Understand that the results of experiments can be obtained over long or short periods or at a distance, using data-logging equipment.	Use information technology to measure the acceleration of a model car as it runs down a ramp; interpret data transmitted by a weather satellite.
	Select and interrogate a computer database to obtain information needed for a task.	Make use of a large database about careers or courses, and refine techniques of enquiry to select relevant information.
	Know when it is appropriate to use a software package for a task rather than other means of information handling.	Consider the usefulness of a computer-aided design package to investigate the ergonomics of kitchen design.
	Understand that dangerous or costly investigations, or those not easily measured, can be simulated by information technology.	Experiment with the operation of a simulated nuclear reactor.
8	Design successful means of collecting information for computer processing.	Design and refine a questionnaire for collecting complex data in a form suitable for analysis by computer; use monitoring and data-logging equipment to record environmental change.
	Select and use software to capture and store data, taking account of retrieval, ease of analysis, and the types of presentation required.	Select and use database or viewdata software to provide information about local amenities.
	Construct a device which responds to data from a sensor; explain how they have made use	Use software to record movement patterns of small mammals, and produce graphs.

Table continued

Level	Statements of attainment	Examples
	of feedback when implementing a system incorporating monitoring and control.	and tables for use in a presentation; develop a robot vehicle which follows a path marked on the ground.
	Use software to represent a situation or process with variables, and show the relationship between them.	Model and investigate the growth of bacteria using a spreadsheet; use a graph-plotting program to find a curve which fits a set of experimental data.
	Understand why electronically stored personal information is potentially easier to misuse than that kept in conventional form.	Evaluate a computer-assisted drafting program used in technology; a graphics package used in art; a desk-top publishing program used in English.
	Design, implement, and document a system for others to use.	Design a system to investigate production schedules and stockholding strategies for a company making and distributing fast foods.
	Understand the effects of inaccurate data in files of personal information.	Research cases where the use of inaccurate data has caused inconvenience; investigate safeguards on access to personal data in computer systems.
10	Decide how to model a system, and design, implement, and test it; justify methods used and choices made.	Develop a system for monitoring the performance of a central-heating system in order to plan a system for a house or school; develop a system for notifying parents that their child's immunization is due.
	Discuss the environmental, ethical, moral, and social issues raised by information technology.	Visit organizations making extensive use of information technology; prepare for the visit by deciding issues to be discussed with employees, such as how information technology was introduced, its effect on their work, and their view of information technology; make

Level	Statements of attainment	Examples
		suggestions about how the introduction of information technology might have been improved.

Note: Pupils unable to communicate by speech, writing, or drawing may use other means, including the use of technology or symbols as alternatives.

Technology: Northern Ireland

The technology curriculum in Northern Ireland is known as 'Technology and Design' and is significantly different from that of England and Wales. Information Technology is a designated cross-curricular theme in the province and so is not linked to technology for assessment purposes as it is on the mainland. There is only one attainment target, Technology and Design Capability, as there is a strong emphasis on the need to consider technological activity as a whole rather than as separate and discrete parts. The attainment targets state that:

Pupils should develop the ability to design products. In particular, they should develop, in parallel, their ability:

- to apply knowledge and understanding;
- to communicate effectively;
- to manipulate a range of materials and components to make products;
- to use energy to drive and control products they design.

The knowledge and understanding which is required in Technology and Design is drawn primarily from Science. Communication of designing emphasizes the use of computers and the strand associated with control emphasizes both electronics and pneumatics as well as computer control. The 'range of materials' includes metal, plastics, textiles, and wood. Food is not a 'material' in the Northern Ireland technology curriculum although Home Economics does have a separate place at key stages 3 and 4. The importance of social, economic, and environmental factors is stressed in every key stage and there is a strong emphasis on the importance of Technology and Design to wealth creation.

History

This section will consider:

- the status of history in the school curriculum across the four key stages, and
- the requirements of the statutory orders.

We begin, however, with a brief summary of some of the issues and controversies surrounding the teaching of history in schools.

Under the 1988 Education Reform Act (England and Wales), history was established as a core foundation subject and as such was to form a compulsory element in the school curriculum for all pupils aged 5–16. This development was welcomed by history teachers as a move which recognized the value of history's contribution to a 'broad and balanced education' and preparation for adult life. Its status under the 1988 Act was the same as the other foundation subjects (modern languages, geography, technology, art, music, and PE).

National Curriculum history has precipitated a great deal of public controversy over *what* history should be taught in schools. This was a subject which produced more controversy and print in the pages of the newspapers and journals than any other, with the possible exception of English. At stake was the place of 'British' history in the school curriculum, together with the place of facts—names, dates, people, and events—in teaching history. On the former it is interesting to consider the different programmes of study for England, Northern Ireland, and Wales, which are summarized below.

Also at the heart of the controversy was the debate around history as 'content' versus 'skills'. The 1970s saw the development of a new rationale for teaching history as teachers and pupils reacted against syllabuses which were chronological outline surveys of British political history. This 'new' history emphasized historical methodology and a syllabus which was 'relevant' to the lives of young people. Modern world history and local history were introduced, together with an emphasis on enquiry-based learning.

Critics of the 'new' history saw the subject being reduced to an endless stream of source evaluation and empathy exercises which paid no attention to historical facts. Critics of 'facts' in history argued that this would simply reduce history to a game of mastermind. This dichotomy between historical skills and facts is, in fact, a false one. Facts, that is, names, dates, events, etc., provide information about the past which is an essential part of history, but they do not in themselves constitute history or provide an understanding of the past. Any study of history needs to include both, that is, a thorough knowledge of past events, together with an understanding of historical method (the way in which historians carry out their work). History also crucially involves a range of explanations and understandings.

This view of school history is the one outlined by the history working group for England. When the statutory orders for history emerged in 1990, they showed considerable continuity with the developments which had taken place in teaching history during the previous two decades.

The position of history in the school curriculum: the current situation

History and the National Curriculum (England and Wales)

Under the terms of the 1988 Education Reform Act (England and Wales), history was a compulsory element in the curriculum at key stages 1, 2, 3, and 4, although there was the option at key stage 4 of following either a long course (equivalent to the time currently allocated to the study of GCSE—10 per cent of the timetable), or a short course which would amount to 5 per cent of the timetabled time.

The review of the national curriculum carried out in 1993 decided that history should become an optional part of the Key Stage Four curriculum. Many historians saw this as a step back reducing the status of the subject and undermining the principles of a national 'entitlement' curriculum. The pressure to allow greater choice at Key Stage 4, and particularly the stress on introducing vocational courses into the curriculum made some reduction in the compulsory core inevitable.

The requirements of the statutory orders

The format of the National Curriculum history is similar to the orders for the other subjects in that it lays down the programmes of study and the attainment targets. However, there are some main differences which need to be taken into account when planning history.

The attainment targets

The history attainment targets are content-free, and identify the concepts and skills of historical methodology. Unlike the attainment targets in other subjects—geography, for example—there are no facts or dates in the attainment targets. All the attainment targets require pupils to demonstrate their knowledge of the content and terminology outlined in the programmes of study. The attainment targets, then, are 'what history is all about', and it is with these that teachers need to start their planning of history at all key stages. There are some differences in the statutory requirements between England, Wales, and Northern Ireland, and these are illustrated below.

Attainment target 1

Wales	Northern Ireland	England
Knowledge and Understanding of History.	Knowledge and Understanding of History.	Knowledge and Understanding of History.

Wales	Northern Ireland	England
This has three strands: (a) change, (b) causation, and (c) different features of a historical situation.	This has three strands: (a) change, (b) causation, and (c) different features of a historical situation.	This has three strands: (a) change, (b) causation, and (c) different features of a historical situation.

Attainment target 2

Wales	Northern Ireland	England
Interpretations of History.	Understanding Points of View.	Interpretations of History.

Attainment target 3

Wales	Northern Ireland	England
The use of Historical Sources.	Acquiring and Evaluating Historical Information.	The use of Historical Sources.

The attainment targets can be summarized as follows:

Hi1. Knowledge and Understanding of History:

Strand A. Change and Continuity: This strand is about recognizing, describing, and analysing change. It involves knowing about different kinds of change and understanding how change can vary in pace and complexity. It is about the nature of progress. It requires an increasingly sophisticated knowledge of chronology and of features of periods of the past.

Strand B. Cause and Consequences: This strand is about analysing and explaining historical events and actions. It involves recognizing causes which should be interpreted broadly to include motive and intention, distinguishing between different types of cause and consequence, understanding how they vary in importance, and appreciating the complexity of the links between them. It requires an increasingly mature ability to select and apply relevant knowledge in support of a convincing argument.

Strand C. Knowing about and Understanding Key Features of Past Situations: This strand is about developing knowledge and understanding and an awareness of different historical periods, societies, situations, and events. It involves acquiring knowledge and understanding of, and comparing the features of, past times and the attitudes and values of people in past societies.

Hi2. Interpretations of History: This attainment target is about recognizing that the past is depicted in many different ways, understanding how different interpretations of past developments or events have come about, and evaluating different interpretations. It involves a knowledge and understanding of past events and situations, the different types of interpretations that exist, the factors that shape interpretations, and the way interpretations may be used to serve social or political purposes.

Hi3. The Use of Historical Sources: This attainment target is about acquiring evidence and drawing inferences from sources and making judgements about their reliability and value. It involves finding out about the past from different types of historical source, and bringing knowledge of the period to bear on the use of sources. In using sources, pupils will be concerned with the provenance of the sources as well as with their content.

The programmes of study

For England, Wales, and Northern Ireland, the programmes of study are arranged in study units.

General requirements of the programmes of study

Within the programmes of study there are also general requirements, which identify key elements which apply to all the history study units across each key stage. These aspects of teaching history also apply to Wales and Northern Ireland and include the following features.

Pupils should be taught history from a variety of perspectives:

- political;
- economic, technological, and scientific;
- social;
- religious, cultural, and aesthetic.

Pupils should also have the opportunity to use a range of historical sources including:

- documents and printed sources;
- artefacts;
- pictures, photographs, and films;
- music;
- oral accounts;
- buildings and sites;
- computer-based materials.

Attention has to be given to cultural diversity in teaching history and there is a requirement that pupils are taught about the social, cultural, religious, and ethnic diversity of societies studied and the experiences of men and women in these societies.

There are different history study units with the programmes of study for England, Wales, and Northern Ireland. These are summarized below.

Northern Ireland

Key stage 1

At key stage 1, as in England and Wales, the programme of study consists of one history study unit. This introduces pupils to the idea of the past through stories, artefacts, visual material, and the study of their personal histories and home life, and the study of changes in the recent past in relation to their parents, grandparents, and their own locality.

At key stages 2 and 3 there are two types of history study units (HSUs): the core study units covering selected areas of Irish, British, European, and world history which must be taught in chronological sequence, and the school-designed history study units (SDUs). The planning of these is left to the school in order to allow teachers to draw on their own particular knowledge and enthusiasms, but they have to meet specified ground rules to ensure compatibility with the HSUs.

Key stage 2

There are six history study units, comprising three compulsory core history study units and three school-designed units. The core study units are:

- Life in Early Times;
- The Vikings;
- Life in Victorian Times.

The school-designed units are:

- a study in development—for example Transport through the Ages.
- a study in depth—for example Aspects of the Roman World.
- a local study—for example a local canal.

Key stage 3

There are seven history study units comprising three compulsory core history study units and four school-designed units. The core study units are:

- (Y8) The Norman Impact on the Medieval World;
- (Y9) Britain, Ireland, and Europe from the late Sixteenth to the early Eighteenth Centuries.

- (Y10) Ireland and British Politics in the late Nineteenth and the early Twentieth Centuries.

The school-designed units are:

- a study in depth, for example The American Frontier.
- a line of development study, for example Energy.
- a local study, for example an archaeological site study, such as Nendrum (linked to an introduction to history and its sources).
- a study related to the twentieth century, for example The Russian Revolution.

(Examples taken from Northern Ireland Curriculum Council— Guidance Materials History, 1991).

Key stage 4

At key stage 4, there are two core history study units:

- Core 1: Northern Ireland and its Neighbours since 1920.
- Core 2: Conflict and Co-operation in Europe since 1919.

Wales

Key stage 1

At key stage 1, as in England and Wales, the programme of study consists of one history study unit. This introduces pupils to the idea of the past through stories, artefacts, visual material, and the study of their personal histories and home life, and the study of changes in the recent past in relation to their parents, grandparents, and their own locality.

Key stage 2

There are four (or five) core study units, two supplementary study units, and two (or one) local history/short time span unit(s). The core study units are:

- Early Peoples: Prehistoric, Celtic, and Roman Britain;
- Invaders and Settlers;
- Life in Tudor and Stuart Times;
- Wales and Britain in Victorian Times.

The supplementary study units are:

- Houses and Households;
- Sailors and Ships;
- Writing and Reading;
- Food and Farming;
- Land and Air Transport since c.1750;
- Crafts in Past Societies;
- Castles, Monasteries, and Parish Churches;
- An Ancient Civilization.

A local/short time span study, for example a local Victorian study, is also included.

The emphasis of the programme of study is on social history within the framework of important developments in Welsh, British, and world history. Pupils should be given the opportunity to build on their understanding of chronology and change as they study selected periods of history. (Non-statutory guidance—History, CCW, 1991)

Key stage 3

There are seven history study units. The four core study units are taught in chronological order. There is then a choice of two from eight supplementary study units and one local history unit.

The emphasis is on the political, economic, social, and cultural aspects of the histories of Wales and Britain, and, where appropriate, the experiences of different countries and societies should be compared with each other.

The core study units are:

- (Y7)—Wales and Britain in the Medieval World;
- (Y8)—Wales and Britain in the Early Modern World;
- (Y9)—Wales in Industrial Britain;
- (Y9)—Britain, Europe, and the World.

The supplementary study units (Exploration and Encounters) are:

- War and Society;
- The World of Work;
- Revolutions;
- Frontiers;

- Migration and Emigration;
- Empires;
- Sport and Society.

A local history study unit is also included.

Key stage 4

Pupils should be taught Welsh or Welsh and British History in the twentieth-century European and world context as appropriate.

Pupils study two units:
(*a*) Wales and Britain in the twentieth century;
(*b*) Understanding the modern world
   (i) The Second World War and its aftermath, together with one of the following themes/developments:
   Democracy in a modern society
   Multi-cultural societies
   The changing status of women
   Scientific and technological developments since 1945.

Model B at KS4

Pre-1900 Welsh or Welsh and British History. Pupils are asked to revisit and investigate a period of history studied at key stage 2 or 3 to build upon their knowledge of Welsh or Welsh and British History.

England

Key stage 1

At key stage 1, as in Northern Ireland and Wales, the programme of study consists of one history study unit. This introduces pupils to the idea of the past through stories, artefacts, visual material, and the study of their personal histories and home life, and the study of changes in the recent past in relation to their parents, grandparents, and their own locality.

Key stage 2

Pupils should be taught nine history study units, which may be combined by schools in different ways. Either five or six core study units must be chosen from:

- Invaders and Settlers: Romans, Anglo-Saxons, and Vikings in Britain;

- Tudors and Stuarts;
- Victorian Britain;
- Britain since 1930;
- Ancient Greece;
- Exploration and Encounters 1450–1550.

Supplementary study units consist of either three or four units, which should complement or extend the core study units. One to be chosen from:

- Ships and Seafarers;
- Food and Farming;
- Houses and Places of Worship;
- Writing and Printing;
- Land Transport, Domestic Life, Families, and Childhood.

A unit based on local history must be included; where two units are chosen from this category, they should involve the study of different types of local history. A further unit must be chosen from:

- Ancient Egypt;
- Mesopotamia;
- Assyria;
- The Indus Valley;
- The Maya;
- Benin.

Key stage 3

There are eight history study units. Five of these are core history study units and three are supplementary study units. The content is prescribed for the core study units:

1. The Roman Empire;
2. Medieval Realms: Britain 1066 to 1500;
3. The Making of the UK: Crowns, Parliaments, and Peoples 1500–1750;
4. Expansion, Trade, and Industry: Britain 1750–1900;
5. The Era of the Second World War.

The core study units 2, 3, 4, and 5 have to be taught chronologically, with at least one core study unit being studied in each of the three years 7, 8, and 9.

The content is not prescribed for the supplementary study units, but there are three categories. These are given in the orders as follows:

1. A unit which extends the study of the core British units for this key stage and:
   - relates to the history of the British Isles before 1920;
   - must either be a study in depth or a theme over a long period of time. Example: The Role of Women in History.

   This can be on local history.

2. A unit involving the study of an episode or turning-point in European history, before 1914, which should:
   - be based on an episode or turning-point of major historical significance;
   - illustrate the links between developments in different parts of Europe;
   - examine the short- and long-term impact of the episode or turning-point.

   Example: The Crusades.

3. A unit involving the study of a past non-European society. This unit should:
   - focus on the key historical issues concerning people of non-European background in a past society in Asia, Africa, or Australasia;
   - involve study from a variety of perspectives: political, economic, technological and scientific, religious, cultural, and aesthetic;
   - be based on a society or societies different from those listed in category C of the programme of study for key stage 2.

(This is based on *History in the National Curriculum*, England, HMSO, 1991.)

Key stage 4

The short course at key stage 4 requires the study of one study unit: Britain, Europe, and the World. The long course at key stage 4 requires the study of the core study unit as above with the addition of two supplementary study units covering a thematic unit designed to deepen pupils' understanding of chronology and to build on historical studies from earlier key stages.

Geography

Geography, like other subjects in the National Curriculum, can be the subject of lively national debate. Some of the critics of contemporary education, here and abroad, have pointed to children's inadequate knowledge of countries and cities as evidence of declining standards. At the same time, others have pointed to the futility of what has been termed a 'capes and bays' approach to the subject. The ability to reel off a list of capital cities or major rivers, it is argued, is as empty an exercise as giving the dates of kings and queens. Inevitably the National Curriculum in geography attracted some of this debate, although in a more muted form than in subjects such as English or history.

The context of and approach to teaching geography have undergone significant changes in the last few decades. Many parents will remember drawing detailed regional maps, with symbols to show where coal mines or shoe manufacturing existed. They might also remember diagrams of V-shaped valleys gouged out by the ice of a glacial period. An interest in regions and the physical characteristics of the earth still exists, but in the context of some new perspectives that have profoundly influenced the way the subject is approached. There have been, for example, some important developments to strengthen the scientific and particularly mathematical basis of the subject. Secondly, in a contrasting but complementary way, there has been a move to focus on issues and problems that go beyond the particular characteristics of regions or countries. The decline in world stocks of natural fuel resources, poverty across significant parts of the globe, and the economic interdependence between developed and underdeveloped countries would be three examples.

A contemporary definition of the subject was made by the working group which prepared the National Curriculum geography report.

1. Geography explores the relationship between the Earth and its peoples through the study of *place*, *space*, and *environment*. Geographers ask the questions *where* and *what*; also *how* and *why*.

2. The study of *place* seeks to describe and understand not only the location of the physical and human features of the Earth,

but also the processes, systems, and interrelationships that create or influence those features.

3. The study of *space* seeks to explore the relationships between places and patterns of activity arising from the use people make of the physical settings where they live and work.

4. The study of the *environment* embraces both its physical and human dimensions. Thus it addresses the resources, sometimes scarce and fragile, that the Earth provides, and on which all life depends; the impact on those resources of human activities; and the wider social, economic, political, and cultural consequences of the interrelationship between the two.

The final version of National Curriculum geography represented in the statutory orders set out five attainment targets:

AT1.   Geographical Study;
AT2.   Knowledge and Understanding of Places;
AT3.   Physical Geography;
AT4.   Human Geography;
AT5.   Environmental Geography.

The description of the knowledge and understanding required at level 1 (the first year of primary schooling), level 4 (when many children will be moving from primary to secondary schooling), and level 10 (the highest level of achievement possible) is set out below

Level	Statements of attainment	Examples
1	Pupils should be able to:	
	(a) Name familiar features of the local area.	Name local landmarks, e.g. roads, postboxes, shops, parks, woods, rivers, hills.
	(b) Identify activities carried out by people in the local area.	Identify activities carried out by parents and people who work in the school, or who visit the school; people who provide a service in the community.
	(c) State where they live.	State the number of dwelling, name of street, and name of the town, district, or village.
	(d) Demonstrate an awareness of the world beyond their local area.	Talk about and paint pictures of places they have visited or seen photographs of.

Level		Statements of attainment	Examples
	(e)	Name the country in which they live.	Know that they live in England.
4	(a)	Name the features marked on Maps B and D at the end of the programmes of study.	
	(b)	Describe how the landscape of a locality outside the local area has been changed by human actions.	Describe major landscape changes associated with economic activities, e.g. farming, industry, quarrying, tourism, and with the development of settlements and communications.
	(c)	Give an account of a recent or proposed change in a locality.	Summarize a redevelopment proposal, e.g. the construction of a bypass or other land-use development, the construction of a housing estate or supermarket, the destruction of part of a rainforest, the flooding of land caused by the construction of a dam.
	(d)	Describe the geographical features of the home region.	Describe the main features, including landscape, distribution of population, and patterns of settlement.
	(e)	Describe how the daily life of a locality in an economically developing country is affected by its landscape, weather, and wealth.	Describe how family life, housing, clothing, and diet in a locality are affected by landscape, weather, and wealth.
10	(a)	Synthesize patterns, relationships, and processes in the home region.	Give a balanced and detailed geographical account of the home region, which explains how the characteristic geographical features, patterns, and processes in the region are interrelated and the extent to which these relationships give coherence to the region.

Table continued

Level	Statements of attainment	Examples
(b)	Evaluate alternative government policies and strategies relevant to the theme selected for 9(a).	Evaluate alternative strategies which are intended to influence agriculture, population movement, and tourism, by assessing their likely consequences.
(c)	Evaluate the significance of foreign investment, loans, and development assistance programmes in the economic development of an economically developing country specified in the programme study.	Appraise the overall effect of foreign investments, loans, and development assistance programmes on the economic development of a country and the effects on different sectors of the economy.
(d)	Analyse recent trends in patterns of international trade and suggest likely future trends.	Explain the growing importance of trade between countries of the Pacific Rim, the significance of trade between countries of the European Community, and between the European Community and other parts of the world; suggest which of these developments are likely to continue to be significant and why.

Note: Pupils unable to communicate by speech, writing, or drawing may use other means including the use of technology, signing systems, or symbols as alternatives.

Modern foreign languages in the National Curriculum

For the first time in its history, MFL is shedding its élitist image. Pupils of all levels of attainment between the ages of 11 and 16 are enjoying a wider-reaching and more varied diet of activities than ever before. Foreign languages are at last, in this multilingual society in which we live, being given the status they deserve. One major factor in this recognition is their inclusion as a foundation subject in the National Curriculum. In effect, this requires all pupils aged between 11 and 16 to study a foreign language, and, though this has resourcing and staffing implications which have yet to be resolved, it is seen as a very positive step forward by teachers of MFL.

Traditionally, the language most frequently offered by schools as a first foreign language has been French. Recently government resources have been invested in changing this state of affairs in favour of a much more diverse pattern, and now it is not unusual to find schools which have 'diversified' offering German, Italian, or Spanish as a first foreign language. Yet concerns about staffing these hitherto lesser-taught languages are far from resolved, since the majority of linguists entering the teaching profession are still French graduates. The issue of pupils changing schools, with a resultant change of foreign language, is also potentially problematic.

Schools are required by the National Curriculum order to offer their pupils a European Community language and may, in addition, offer a non-European Community language. Nineteen languages from which schools may choose are listed (those asterisked are official European Community languages): Arabic, Bengali, Chinese (Cantonese or Mandarin), Danish*, French*, German*, Greek (modern)*, Gujarati, Hebrew (modern), Hindi, Italian*, Japanese, Punjabi, Portuguese*, Russian, Spanish*, Turkish, Urdu.

The order

In common with each subject, the order for the National Curriculum for MFL contains attainment targets which set out the learning objectives of pupils in key stages 3 and 4, and an accompanying programme of study prescribing the course of study which pupils must follow in order to achieve the attainment targets.

Attainment targets

These represent the framework through which the programmes of study will be assessed. There are four attainment targets for MFL:

AT1. Listening;
AT2. Speaking;
AT3. Reading;
AT4. Writing.

(AT1 for Irish in Irish-medium education is entitled Watching and Listening so that it is consistent with key stages 1 and 2).

Each attainment target is divided into levels, which are described by a series of statements of attainment. These statements are the criteria by which a pupil's language skills are assessed. All four attainment targets apply at both key stages 3 and 4. However, there are two models of assessment which come into play at key stage 4.

Model A: 'for pupils at Key Stage 3 and those in Key Stage 4 *following a single subject GCSE course*'. These pupils will be assessed in all four attainment targets.

Model B: 'for pupils in Key Stage 4 **not** *following a single subject GCSE course*'. These pupils will be assessed in any two attainment targets.

This means that, although all pupils are required to study a foreign language from the age of II to 16, at key stage 4 pupils are not necessarily required to study up to GCSE level. This has caused concern to many teachers, who fear that some pupils may be disadvantaged by not being given access to a full GCSE course and that shorter non-GCSE will have low status and be seen as being of little value.

The programmes of study

These define the essential learning experiences all pupils should have together with the teaching content. They are divided into two parts:

Part 1: Learning and Using the Target Language ('target' language is now a commonly used phrase). This describes the skills which should be developed through activities in the target language.

Part 2: Areas of Experience. This sets out the content of the MFL curriculum as contexts which should be explored through the target language.

These are not intended to be seen as two separate components but as being mutually dependent on each other, Part 1 being the means through which the content (Part 2) should be presented and learnt.

Part 1: Learning and Using the Target Language

There are six skill areas which pupils should develop:

1. communicating in the target language (mainly through speaking and writing);

2. understanding and responding (mainly but not exclusively through listening and speaking);
3. language-learning skills and awareness of language;
4. cultural awareness;
5. the ability to work with others;
6. the ability to learn independently.

Each of the skill areas is prefaced with the phrase 'In learning and using the target language, pupils should have regular opportunities to . . . ' and then a series of activities is listed. For example, for skill area 3:

In learning and using the target language, pupils should have regular opportunities to:

- learn phrases by heart;
- learn (and at times recite) short texts (e.g. rhymes, poems, songs, jokes, or tongue-twisters);
- learn how sounds are represented in writing;
- develop their awareness of the different conventions of the written and spoken language;
- increase their awareness of different language forms and registers;
- use knowledge about language (linguistic patterns, structures, grammatical features and relationships, and compound words and phrases) to infer meaning and develop their own use of language;
- infer meaning;
- interpret in both directions between the target language and another language (e.g. interpret between two people speaking different languages).

In undertaking these activities, pupils may produce evidence of achievement in all of the four attainment targets (listening, speaking, reading, and writing) which may be recorded by the teacher. Certainly it is not intended that results from all activities be recorded. This would lead to the undesirable situation where teachers were teaching solely in order to assess, and would undermine much of the progress which has been made by teachers in setting up activities which are both motivating and worthwhile in themselves.

In the Northern Ireland orders Part 1 of the programmes of study is divided into 'general skills', and 'language-specific skills'. The language-specific skills are similar to those outlined in the English and Welsh orders but the general skills include:

- personal and social skills;
- transferable learning skills;
- vocational skills.

These are not separated in the English and Welsh orders but are largely subsumed under the heading 'Learning and Using the Target Language'.

Part 2: Areas of Experience

As already mentioned, this is the part of the National Curriculum for MFL which outlines the context and content of the learning experiences to be offered to pupils. There are seven areas of experience in the English and Welsh orders:

Area A: Everyday Activities;
Area B: Personal and Social Life;
Area C: The World around Us;
Area D: The World of Education, Training, and Work;
Area E: The World of Communications;
Area F: The International World;
Area G: The World of Imagination and Creativity.

In Northern Ireland these are known as contexts for learning, of which there are six:

A: Everyday Activities;
B: Personal Life and Social Relationships;
C: The World around Us;
D: The World of Work;
E: The World of Communications and Technology;
F: The International World.

Each context lists a number of topics which learners should have the opportunity to cover. Each of these areas (in both orders) must be studied by each pupil at least once in each key stage, though each time the AoE is 'visited' the topic and the language taught need to be broadened and enriched rather than repeated. Every area is illustrated by a number of examples appropriate to key stages 3 and 4. These are not prescriptive but offer guidance to teachers in very broad statements. For example:

Area A: Everyday activities.

During each Key Stage pupils should have regular opportunities to explore in the target language topics which deal with activities they are likely to engage in at home and school. This should include the language of the classroom. Examples of topics:

- home life
- daily routines
- shopping
- food and drink
- going out
- leisure activities and sport
- youth culture
- school life
- school holidays   (DES, MFL in the National Curriculum: 27)

This allows for flexibility, since none of the examples anywhere in the order is statutory; but the order does state categorically that topics should:

- be relevant to pupils' needs and interests;
- give pupils a good insight into each area of experience at a breadth and depth matched to their individual capabilities, maturity, and interests;
- provide opportunities for comparisons between the pupils' own way of life and that of the other language community;
- be planned and taught in a way which helps pupils develop the knowledge, understanding, and skills needed to progress through the levels of attainment in each attainment target;

and that through the areas of experience pupils should have opportunities in each key stage to:

- explore links with other subjects;
- develop knowledge, understanding, and skills related to cross-curricular dimensions and themes;
- extend their knowledge and understanding of the language, linguistic conventions, and culture of the country or communities where the target language is spoken.

There has been some debate as to the wisdom of separating out The World of Imagination and Creativity as an area of experience in its own right. Many teachers argue that it should permeate all of the other areas and therefore do not tackle it as an isolated area.

There is very little specific reference to the teaching of grammar in the order. Since it covers nineteen different languages the working party felt it inappropriate to define specific structures and grammatical points to be covered at particular levels. The most specific statement is in the programmes of study Part 1: Developing Language Learning Skills and Awareness of Language, which is quoted above. However, in their final report to the Secretary of State the working party advise that teachers:

use major structures frequently in familiar contexts and with known vocabulary . . . Similarly, once a structure has been practised . . . it is essential that learners should be regularly provided with realistic situations in which it is natural to use and thus consolidate it . . . Learners of all abilities are much more likely to be able to grasp and work with grammatical structures if these are presented not through formal exposition but through demonstrations which make a strong visual or aural impression and require an active response. (DES, MFL for ages 11 to 16: 56)

The working party final report

As with other subject areas the Secretary of State, in drawing up the order, consulted a group of advisers, who in turn drew up a final report. The report's recommendations were based on as wide a consultation with teachers and teacher educators as possible in the short time allowed. This report details some features which may be evident in a classroom where the requirements of the National Curriculum languages are being addressed:

- the target language is the normal means of communication;
- activities are well matched to learners' age and abilities;
- learners are clear about what they are doing;
- activities are varied and taken at an appropriate pace;
- activities bring a range of skills into play;
- learners often work co-operatively in groups;
- learners become increasingly independent in their work;
- published course materials are used selectively;
- some activities are planned in collaboration with other departments;
- learners read extensively for information and pleasure;
- learners are given an insight into both their own and the foreign culture;

- learners have regular contacts with foreign speakers;
- assessment is integrated with teaching and learning;
- homework is a planned part of the course.

Under the National Curriculum and influenced by the findings of this report, teachers are developing approaches which take into account how pupils learn languages. There is an emphasis on using the target language for all classroom business so that pupils begin to see languages not so much as a school subject but as a real and effective equivalent to their mother tongue. Pupils are being encouraged, by developing skills of language awareness and language analysis, to become more independent as linguists. Teachers are developing resources and teaching strategies to motivate all levels of learner. This is a challenging innovation but investment of time and teachers' dedication is resulting in a promising rise in the up-take of languages in post-16 study.

Art

Art, along with music and physical education, was in the final group of subjects to be set out in statutory orders laid before Parliament in March 1992. The plans for art had been received with very little controversy. There had been disagreements between the Department for Education and the art working group on the number of attainment targets, but the broad principles of art education had been accepted. The National Curriculum has two attainment targets in England:

AT1. Investigating and Making;
AT2. Knowledge and Understanding;

whereas in Welsh schools the Secretary of State for Wales decided to keep the threefold structure proposed in the working party report. The three attainment targets are titled Understanding, Making, and Investigating.

The working party that prepared the recommendations for art within the National Curriculum recognized that, in primary schools, art is usually taught by general class teaching. In cases of best practice, they suggest, the head and teachers share aims and objectives, often expressed in a clearly stated policy document. The continuity provided by individual teachers planning within that agreed policy is an important factor. In the most successful schools, the place of art education in the curriculum is understood and appropriate teaching and organisation provided. In particular, the staff:

- stimulate pupils' imgination and inventiveness; for example, making classrooms visually stimulating, and providing enrichment from displays, books, works and visits by artists, craftworkers and designers;
- give clear guidance, where appropriate, having analysed the steps that pupils need to take to gain a skill or understand a concept;
- provide opportunities for pupils to develop proficiency in a limited range of hand tools and materials, both traditional and new, while avoiding the superficiality which can come from working with too diverse an array of art materials and techniques;
- ensure that pupils produce work in both two and three dimensions—the latter being particularly important for tactile learning, understanding of scale and proportion and the handling of tools;
- balance the activity of making art, craft and design with opportunities for pupils to reflect upon and discuss their own work and the work of others;
- develop pupils' drawing abilities to the point where they are at ease using drawing as a tool; for example, to aid thinking;
- develop pupils' confidence, value of and pleasure in art, craft and design;
- appreciate and value pupils' individual responses in their own right, rather than seeing them as a form of inferior adult art.

At the secondary level the report was more critical, and HMI reports were quoted that showed strong contrasts from school to school in what students achieved, and the range of activities provided. Standards in painting, for example, were not as high as in drawing, and in over half the schools surveyed three-dimensional work was restricted to ceramics. Most schools, the report suggested, give inadequate attention to the appreciation and critical judgement of work by artists, craftworkers, and designers. The National Curriculum report goes on to suggest:

The National Curriculum provides an opportunity to bring about important advances in the teaching of art, craft and design in schools.

In many primary and some secondary schools there have been traditional preoccupations which have inhibited the development of a rich and rewarding art curriculum. In these schools, a narrow range of activities has been dominant, centred almost entirely on 'making' and accompanied by an uncritical reliance on pupils possessing instinctive powers of self-expression. Much has been undertaken in the past in the name of personal expressiveness which is neither personal nor expressive. The structured study of the great variety of ideas and technologies of contemporary art and design has been neglected, and insufficient attention has been given to the progressive development of key skills.

In art the statutory orders are only set out in terms of what should be achieved at the end of key stages 1–3. (Art is not prescribed beyond key stage 3.) The attainment targets, programmes of study, and examples for each of the attainment targets at the end of key stage 2 are set out overleaf to illustrate the style and form of the approach adopted.

Attainment target 1: Investigating and Making (key stage 2)

End of key stage statements	Programme of study	Examples
By the end of key stage 2, pupils should be able to:	Pupils should:	Pupils could:
(a) Communicate ideas and feelings in visual form based on what they observe, remember, and imagine.	(i) Select and record images and ideas from first-hand observation.	Make carefully observed drawings around the school—looking up (the sky-line); looking down ('bird's eye view'); looking through (windows, fences, gates, tree branches, hedges).
		Make close and carefully observed drawings of reflections in and around the school; e.g. car bodies, mirrors, windows, puddles, spoons.
	(ii) Respond to memory and imagination using a range of media.	Design and make a model diorama with an underwater theme.
		Recall Sports Day as the starting-point for a collage.
		Work with a simple draw/paint computer system.
		Make a sequence of images to illustrate an incident described in a local newspaper.
	(iii) Use a sketch-book to record observations and ideas.	Sketch things of interest on a school visit.
	(iv) Experiment with ideas suggested by different source materials and explain how they have used them to develop their work.	Collect illustrations from comics, magazines, or other media as a preliminary to making a mask or puppet.
		Collect illustrations and descriptions from books about endangered species.
(b) Develop an idea or theme for their work, drawing on visual and other sources, and discuss their methods.		Discuss with other pupils how to make a visual presentation during school assembly.

End of key stage statements	Programme of study	Examples
(c) Experiment with and apply their knowledge of the elements of art, choosing appropriate media	(v) Apply their knowledge and experience of different materials, tools, and techniques, using them experimentally and expressively.	Experiment with different ways of printing the same image; e.g. sponge rollers and stencils, hard rollers, and polystyrene or card blocks.
	(vi) Experiment with different qualities of line and tone in making images.	Make large-scale portraits in charcoal to depict a character described in a story.
	(vii) Apply the principles of colour mixing in making various kinds of images.	Make paintings of the landscape in which several hues of green are explored.
	(viii) Experiment with pattern and texture in designing and making images and artefacts.	Collect objects with textured surfaces, e.g. bark, nail brush; use similar textures to decorate simple containers in clay.
	(ix) Experiment with ways of representing shape, form, and space.	Take a number of different photographs from the same position, and make a montage to create a sense of space.
	(x) Plan and make three-dimensional structures using various materials and for a variety of purposes.	Make life-sized animals from card by cutting, scoring, folding, and gluing.
(d) Modify their work in the light of its development and their original intentions.	(xi) Adapt or modify their work in order to realize their ideas and explain and justify the changes they have made.	Recognize when they need to use different materials or work on a larger scale to pursue an idea effectively.
	(xii) Use a developing specialist vocabulary to describe their work and what it means.	Describe when and why they would use an orange red (vermilion) rather than a blue red (crimson).

Attainment target 2: Knowledge and Understanding (key stage 2)

End of key stage statements	Programme of study	Examples
By the end of key stage 2, pupils should be able to:	Pupils should:	Pupils could:
(a) Identify different kinds of art and their purposes.	(i) Compare the different purposes of familiar visual forms and discuss their findings with their teachers and peers.	Look at how faces are depicted for a variety of purposes; e.g. portraits, postage stamps, posters, television commercials, gargoyles, etc.
		Make a list of all the things they have at home which they consider to be examples of art.
		Compare the way in which the design of clothes has changed over the centuries or in different cultures and consider some of the reasons for these changes; e.g. sports-wear, uniforms, working and ceremonial clothes.
	(ii) Understand and use subject-specific terms such as landscape, still-life, mural.	Discuss the ways in which artists have depicted the English landscape, using terms such as background, foreground, balance, shade, hue, transparent, sketching.
(b) Begin to identify the characteristics of art in a variety of genres from different periods, cultures, and traditions, showing some knowledge of the related historical background.	(iii) Look at and discuss art from early, Renaissance, and later periods in order to start to understand the way in which art has developed and the contribution of influential artists or groups of artists to that development.	Talk about how subjects are illustrated in Egyptian wall painting, on Greek vases, Assyrian relief panels, and in the Bayeux tapestry.
		Discuss how Breughel the Elder depicted the everyday life of Flemish people in the sixteenth century.

End of key stage statements	Programme of study	Examples
		Compare how nature is represented in Impressionist paintings by Monet, Pissarro, Sisley, Renoir, Degas, with the work of Turner, Constable, and Hiroshige.
	(iv) Identify and compare some of the methods and materials that artists use.	Compare the way that different artists have carved or constructed figures using materials such as stone, clay, plaster, wire; e.g. the work of Michelangelo, Epstein, Hepworth, and Giacometti.
	(v) Experiment with some of the methods and approaches used by other artists, and use these imaginatively to inform their own work.	Develop a drawing they have made of a flower into a design motif for appliqué in fabric and thread; note the different ways in which the flower motif is used in textiles from a variety of cultures and times.
(c) Make imaginative use in their own work of a developing knowledge of the work of other artists.		

Music

Music education has always featured significantly in the life of schools. Many people will remember the 'recorder chorus' of their primary schools and the rather more formal 'lesson a week' that characterized secondary education. Everyone will remember school concerts or the occasional musical event during assembly. Few prize-days or presentation evenings occur without some sort of musical presentation, and many school drama events have a strong musical presence. Many thousands of children have also been able to benefit from individual instrumental tuition. Music, therefore, is more than a subject within the National Curriculum. It is part of the culture and ethos of the school, and many parents and children use the musical profile of the school as one of the touch-stone issues in making a choice of schools.

The working party that prepared the proposals for music in the National Curriculum recognised the importance of music in the curriculum, but, as with the group looking at art, they were critical of wide variations in standards and provision between schools. In primary schools, pupils should, they suggested, be able to develop and refine their listening skills, to extend their experience of singing and playing, and to become involved in improvising and composing. Yet to do this very much depended on the availability of someone on the staff with specialist expertise; and where schools have such expertise, choirs, orchestras, and a high take-up of instrumental tuition is likely to be found.

At secondary level, music is usually taught as a separate subject, where the working party reported that attitudes were generally pos-itive, particularly when opportunities exist to explore a wide range of musical styles. Standards in composing were, however, variable and there was very little liaison between primary and secondary schools in terms of the way the music curriculum was operated. The working party carefully set out the way music teaching in schools should develop:

Music is so much a part of the background of everyday life that we tend to take it for granted. For many people, however, it is a powerful focus for creative energy, and one which both stimulates and guides the imagination. Music education aims to develop aesthetic sensitivity and creative ability in all pupils. For those who show high levels of motivation, commitment and skill, it can lead to employment in the music profession, the music industries and teaching. For many others, who choose different career paths, it can supply the foundation for greatly enriched leisure pursuits, both as listeners and as participants in music-making.

Within that framework, we consider that the main aim of music education in schools is to foster pupils' sensitivity to, and their understanding and enjoyment of, music, through an active involvement in listening, composing and performing. The development of musical perception and skills is dependent upon the quality, range and appropriateness of these musical experiences, as they are provided within and outside school. There are of course many different styles of music, appropriate for different purposes and offering different kinds of satisfaction and challenge; excellence may be found in any style of musical expression.

The study of music as a foundation subject should provide for the progressive development of:

- awareness and appreciation of organised sound patterns;
- skills in movement, such as motor co-ordination and dexterity, vocal skills, and skills in aural imagery (imagining and internalising sounds), acquired through exploring and organising sound;
- sensitive, analytical and critical responses to music;
- the capacity to express ideas, thoughts and feelings through music;
- awareness and understanding of traditions, idioms and musical styles from a variety of cultures, times and places; and
- the experience of fulfilment which derives from striving for the highest possible artistic and technical standards.

As in art, the National Curriculum is set out in key stages, and set out below is what pupils should know in each of the attainment targets at the end of key stage 2.

Attainment target 1: Performing and Composing (key stage 2)

End of key stage statements	Programme of study	Examples
By the end of key stage 2, pupils should be able to:	Pupils should:	Pupils could:
(a) Perform from notations interpreting signs, symbols, and simple musical instructions.	(i) Memorize and internalize songs and musical ideas of increasing length and/or complexity.	Sing back a newly heard phrase played on an instrument.
	(ii) Perform from simple notations and/ or signals and understand a variety of musical instructions.	Accompany a song with an instrumental ostinato from notation which indicates when to play louder and quieter.
(b) Sing and play a range of music, controlling pitch, rhythm, and dynamics.	(iii) Sing an expanding repertoire of songs (unison and simple two-part), and pieces requiring a variety of vocal techniques, with increasing understanding and control of pitch, duration, dynamics, diction, and phrasing.	Sing lullabies or sea-shanties choosing the appropriate vocal qualities.
(c) Perform in a group, maintaining a simple part independently of another group.	(iv) Perform pieces/accompaniments on a widening range of more sophisticated instruments, with increasing dexterity and control of sound.	Perform a percussion accompaniment to a song. Practise and perform an independent part in a group piece, following variations of pace and dynamics.
	(v) Maintain a part as a member of a group in a round or simple part song.	Sing two-part songs and songs with descants.
	(vi) Play an individual instrumental part in a group piece.	Perform a part within a graphic score. Learn from staff notation, and perform, a piece for recorder ensemble.
	(vii) Rehearse and direct to develop skills and improve techniques.	Work in a group to produce a performance for the rest of the class.

End of key stage statements	Programme of study	Examples
	(viii) Plan and present their own projects/performances, being aware of the need to communicate to different audiences.	Discuss and organize the most suitable position for each performer. Plan and present a contribution to a school assembly.
(d) Devise and develop musical ideas within simple structures.	(ix) Explore and use a widening range of sound sources.	Use recorders, keyboards, computers, and electronic equipment when composing.
	(x) Choose specific sounds and combinations of sounds to create a complete musical shape.	Discuss descriptive sounds for a composition based on a poem before experimenting with instruments.
	(xi) Develop musical ideas through improvising, composing, and arranging.	Improvise a solo section in a class piece based on a rondo form (ABACADA) or a vocal 'verse' alternating with a given 'chorus'.
	(xii) Create music in response to a range of stimuli, using appropriate musical structures.	Create a piece in response to a rhythmic pattern, movement, a series of pictures, or first-hand experience such as a visit to a nature trail.
(e) Communicate musical ideas to others and record compositions through the use of notations.	(xiii) Record and communicate musical ideas through notations which define timbre, dynamics, duration, and, where appropriate, pitch.	Make a graphic score of a composition. Work in a group to devise a piece before teaching it to another group.

Attainment target 2: Listening and Appraising (key stage 2)

End of key stage statements	Programme of study	Examples
By the end of key stage 2, pupils should be able to:	Pupils should:	Pupils could:
(a) Listen attentively to music of various kinds, recognizing the main musical elements; distinguishing musical instruments, and responding to changes in character and mood.	(i) Develop their understanding of musical elements, and ability to describe them in appropriate vocabulary, and to interpret some of the signs related to them:	Listen to *Pictures at an Exhibition* by Mussorgsky and consider how sounds, structures, and expressive devices are used to create each picture.
	pitch: melody; chords; duration: pulse; metre and rhythm; pace: gradations of speed; timbre: tone quality of voice/ instruments; texture: melody, accompaniment, polyphony; dynamics: gradations of volume; accents; structure: repetition; contrast; simple forms.	
	(ii) Learn to distinguish the sounds made by a range of instruments, individually and in combination.	Recognize instruments used in *Rodeo* by Copland. Listen to and identify different instruments in a percussion ensemble. Listen to jazz groups and identify solo instruments.

End of key stage statements	Programme of study	Examples
(b) Understand the principal features of the history of music and appreciate a variety of musical traditions.	(iii) Listen to a range of instrumental and vocal music from early, Classical, and later periods.	Listen to examples of medieval dances, a chamber work such as the *Trout* quintet by Schubert, a suite for orchestra such as Holst's *The Planets*, a cantata such as *Carmina Burana* by Orff.
	(iv) Listen to the work of influential composers and learn something of their social and historical context and importance to the development of musical traditions.	Listen to pieces of music by composers such as Bach, Beethoven, Wagner, Vaughan Williams, and Shostakovich and discuss their effects and characteristics.
(c) Describe, discuss, and undertake simple analysis and evaluation of musical compositions and performances.	(v) Talk about music heard in class, including their own compositions and performances.	Explain the initial musical ideas behind an original composition, and how they were developed.
		Explore the way in which musical ideas and themes change and develop within a work heard in the classroom.
		Discuss the reflection of mood in music in passages from Handel's *Messiah* or Debussy's *La Cathédrale engloutie*.

Physical education

PE tends to attract very contrasting responses from children. For some, stimulated and enthused by individual or team sports, it can be the high point of the curriculum. For others it can be just the reverse, particularly where cross-country runs and compulsory showers become part of the experience! The latter, however, is becoming an increasingly rare experience; PE teachers now embrace a very different idea of the subject. The National Curriculum is much more than forward and backward rolls, jumping the horse, or scaling a rope. Look, for example, at what the working group said physical education should seek to achieve.

Physical Education educates young people in and through the use and knowledge of the body and its movement. It:

- develops physical competence and enables pupils to engage in worthwhile physical activities;
- promotes physical development and teaches pupils to value the benefits of participation in physical activity while at school and throughout life;
- develops artistic and aesthetic understanding within and through movement, and
- helps to establish self-esteem through the development of physical confidence and helps pupils to cope with both success and failure in competitive and co-operative physical activities.

Physical Education also contributes to:
- the development of problem solving skills;
- the development of inter-personal skills; and
- the forging of links between the school and the community, and across cultures.

The purposes, it is important to note, are directed towards individual development and the report was at pains to separate out sport or games from the learning that is associated with physical education. Sport can, of course, help to fulfil some of the aims of a full programme of PE, but the two should not be seen as synonymous.

In PE the National Curriculum is defined in terms of just one attainment target. The central importance of *activity* in all its forms is stressed, and six areas are identified in the programme of study:

- games;
- gymnastics;
- dance;
- athletics;
- outdoor and adventurous activities;
- swimming at key stages 1 and 2.

These activities are set out as follows in the programme of study. In athletic activities pupils should:

- practise and develop basic actions in running (over short and longer distances and in relays), throwing, and jumping;
- be given opportunities for and guidance in measuring, comparing, and improving their own performance;
- experience competitions, including those they make up themselves.

In dance, pupils should:

- make dances with clear beginnings, middles, and ends involving improvising, exploring, selecting, and refining content, and sometimes incorporating work from other aspects of the curriculum, in particular music, art, and drama;
- be given opportunities to increase the range and complexity of body actions, including step patterns and use of body parts;
- be guided to enrich their movements by varying shape, size, direction, level, speed, tension, and continuity;
- in response to a range of stimuli, express feelings, moods, and ideas and create simple characters and narratives in movement;
- describe and interpret the different elements of a dance.

In games, pupils should individually, with a partner, and in small groups:

- explore and be guided to an understanding of common skills and principles, including attack and defence, in invasion, net/wall, and striking/fielding games;
- be helped to improve the skills of sending, receiving, and travelling with a ball for invasion, net/wall, and striking/fielding games;
- be given opportunities to develop their own games practices, working towards objectives decided sometimes by themselves and sometimes by the teacher;

- make up, play, and refine their own games within prescribed limits, considering and developing rules and scoring systems.

In gymnastic activities, pupils should:

- be enabled, both on the floor and using apparatus, to find more ways of rolling, jumping, swinging, balancing, and taking weight on hands, and to adapt, practise, and refine these actions;
- be guided to perform in a controlled manner and to understand that the ending of one action can become the beginning of the next;
- be given opportunities both on the floor and using apparatus in response to set tasks, to explore, select, develop, practise, and refine a longer series of actions making increasingly complex movement sequences which they are able to repeat;
- be enabled to respond to a variety of tasks, alone or with a partner, emphasizing changing shape, speed, and direction through gymnastic actions.

In outdoor and adventurous activities, pupils should:

- be taught the principles of safety in the outdoors and develop the ability to assess and respond to challenges in a variety of contexts and conditions;
- experience outdoor and adventurous activities in different environments (such as school grounds and premises, parks, woodlands, or sea shore) that involve planning, navigation, working in small groups, recording, and evaluating;
- be taught the skills necessary for the activity undertaken with due regard for safety including the correct use of appropriate equipment.

In swimming, pupils should:

- be taught the codes of hygiene and courtesy for using swimming pools;
- be given opportunities to develop confidence in water; be taught how to rest in water, how to float, and to adopt support positions;
- be taught a variety of means of propulsion using either arms or legs or both, and develop effective and efficient swimming strokes on front and back;

- be taught the principles and skills of water safety and assess the nature, visibility, and location of water hazards in a variety of conditions;
- be taught survival skills appropriate to their competence in water and be encouraged to evaluate their own abilities and limitations.

The end-of-key stage statements of 'what pupils should be able to do' are couched in very general terms. Six statements, for example, are given for the end of key stage 2; by the end of the key stage, pupils should be able to:

1. plan, practise, improve, and remember more complex sequences of movement;
2. perform effectively in activities requiring quick decision-making;
3. respond safely, alone and with others, to challenging tasks, taking account of levels of skill and understanding;
4. swim unaided at least 25 metres and demonstrate an understanding of water safety;
5. evaluate how well they and others perform and behave against criteria suggested by the teacher, and suggest ways of improving performance;
6. sustain energetic activity over appropriate periods of time in a range of physical activities, and understand the effects of exercise on the body.

Physical education has been one of the less controversial areas of the National Curriculum. There remain, however, a number of issues that regularly attract media attention. The contribution of PE to the general health of the country, and health education specifically, is often discussed. If schools can develop a positive attitude to exercise and activity, the benefits could be considerable. How appropriate PE is to the development of boys and girls is also an issue. Should they be taught together or separately? What should be our attitude towards girls' rugby teams? Should we try to convince boys of the value of contemporary dance? Finally, a third example relates to the performance of national teams. If the national football team fails to qualify for the World Cup, or if the Ashes are continuously lost to the Australians, are the schools to blame?

It is inevitable that these debates will continue. Significantly, however, the National Curriculum has acknowledged a broad interpretation of what physical education represents. This, in itself, offers an entitlement to opportunity for young people to join personal motivation and satisfaction in a broader range of activity than has traditionally been the case.

7 Special Needs

Many people are now aware that the school provision for children with special needs underwent revolutionary changes in the 1980s and early 1990s. The impetus came from a report on the education of handicapped children and young people published in 1978 (the Warnock Report). This established clearly that educational goals should be the same for all young people, regardless of any disability they might have. In 1981 an Education Act was passed, and in the following decade children with special educational needs who had been educated separately were gradually integrated into mainstream schools. Special schools still exist, but for a very small minority of children.

The 1978 Warnock Report and the Education Acts (1981 and 1993) reflected the change in social attitudes to disability that has characterized the latter part of the twentieth century. Segregation in special schools had done little for the progress or self-esteem of many children; nor did it help promote sensitive, informed, and caring understanding on the part of children or adults without disability.

Children who experience particular difficulties may be assessed and where appropriate become the subject of what is termed a statement. With the agreement and, following the 1993 Act, the full involvement of parents throughout the process, this will be drawn up by a group of professionals from a variety of backgrounds (educational psychologists, doctors, social workers, and teachers). When the statement is complete, the school may receive extra resources to support the child's education. It will certainly be required to follow the recommendation made in the statement. In drawing up the statement, careful consideration will be given to the extent to which the child can follow the National Curriculum. The Schools Curriculum and Assessment Authority has made it very clear that children with special needs should have maximum access to all aspects of the National Curriculum. Only when this is clearly impossible will the requirements be waived (the rather unfriendly technical term *disapplication* is used in the legislation to describe this process). Whatever the outcome, the curriculum programme for each child will need to be broad, balanced, and rich in opportunities for a full range of activities.

There will also be pupils in schools who are not the subject of a statement but who still have special educational needs. They too will need support. These children include those who follow the full National Curriculum programme of their peers but require specialist help with reading or numbers, and those who have been temporarily withdrawn from all or parts of the National Curriculum. This latter situation will only occur in a few circumstances, for example:

- where pupils have arrived from such a different educational system that they require a period of adjustment to the National Curriculum;
- where pupils have had spells in hospital, been educated at home, or been excluded from school and need time to adjust;
- where pupils have temporary severe emotional problems (perhaps because of a family crisis) and need special arrangements.

The headteacher, with the agreement of the governors, has the power to make what is called a temporary 'general direction' to waive part of the National Curriculum. This cannot be done for longer than six months. The school is still responsible for the child's curriculum and it must ensure that a broad and balanced range of activities is offered.

All schools are now required to draw up policies for teaching and supporting children with special needs. School prospectuses and governors' statements about the curriculum will include a reference to the approach adopted. Governors must report once a year to parents and this report must include a statement on the school's special needs policy. In recent years there has been a marked shift not only towards teaching special-needs children in mainstream schools, but also towards teaching them in ordinary classes. OFSTED inspections particularly address special needs provision. Teachers with particular responsibilities for special-needs children are therefore more likely to be working alongside their colleagues, giving group and individual support, rather than in their own specialist room or department.

Teachers, governors, and parents should consider carefully the sorts of issues that inform the development of a special-needs policy for the curriculum. In one of the first National documents on this issue (*A Curriculum for All*—see Further Reading) schools were asked to develop responses to a number of questions. Examples included:

- Can the tasks and activities for any one attainment level be chosen and presented to enable children with a wide range of attainments to experience success? For instance, emphasis on oral rather than written work will help some pupils with learning difficulties.
- Can activities be matched to pupils' differing paces and styles of learning, interests, capabilities, and previous experience; can time and order of priority be allocated accordingly?
- Can the activities be broken down into a series of small and achievable steps for pupils who have marked learning difficulties?
- Will the activities stretch pupils of whom too little may have been expected in the past? These pupils are likely to include some with physical, sensory, or other impairment who are high attainers.
- Can a range of communication methods be used with pupils with language difficulties?
- Will the purpose of the activities and the means of achieving them be understood and welcomed by pupils with learning difficulties?

The school environment plays an important role in developing the learning of all pupils, but it is especially important for children with special needs. The layout of the classroom, the capacity to change the way pupils are grouped, the provision of information technology and other resources, and the encouragement of co-operative approaches to learning amongst pupils can all support the integration of children with special needs into the curriculum, and stimulate their capacity to learn.

The advice in *A Curriculum for All* gives numerous ideas and examples of how subject teaching in the National Curriculum can be sensitive to children with special needs. For example:

- *Use of language*: 'Without water human beings are unable to survive' could become 'People need water to live.'

- *Practical activities*: Pupils may be given paper for folding into a windmill shape. Those with learning difficulties might need to have the shape printed on the sheet with the folds marked. For a visually impaired pupil the lines can be indented in the paper with pressure from a ball pen or a spur-wheel available from the Royal National Institute for the Blind (RNIB). This creates an embossed shape on the reverse side of the paper which the child can feel. Even with extra help like this, pupils will still need close guidance by the class teacher and classroom helpers.
- *Classroom method*: Teachers will need to find ways to help those pupils who have specific learning difficulties in reading and writing to make use of their oral strengths (for example, use of tape-recorder and word-processor) and to ensure that evaluation and feedback on work are not over-dominated by handwritten products.

It is important that everyone involved, professionals, parents, and governors, is fully aware of the statutory responsibilities and regulations in formulating and developing policies. For example, the statutory orders for key stage 1 in English allow pupils to be exempted from the 'Handwriting' requirements if they need to use a non-sighted form of writing or if they have such a degree of physical disability that the attainment target is impossible. This has implications for the way in which National Curriculum achievements are assessed and reported to parents. SCAA gives specific advice on how the regulations should be interpreted, and local education authorities also have officers and advisers who monitor the way the National Curriculum is taught in schools and can give individual advice to parents and teachers of children with special educational needs.

8 Parents and Governors

Parents

One of the main purposes of the 1988 Education Reform Act was to provide parents with a wider choice of schools. Whether this has been achieved, or indeed whether it is desirable, is the cause of much debate. One consequence of the Act, however, is the existence of numerous statutory requirements to make available to parents information about the school's and their own child's curriculum. Some of these requirements were introduced in earlier Education Acts, in 1981 and 1986.

Those who want to find out as much as possible about a school curriculum can:

1. obtain copies of the statutory orders for each of the subjects: these are contained in loose-leaf folders. Every school[1] must have these available for parents to look through, and they can also be purchased through HMSO (see Further Reading);
2. ask for a copy of the school prospectus, which should contain the governors' statement of curriculum aims for the school;
3. look through the school prospectus for the following information which must be included:

   - a summary of the content and organization of that part of the curriculum relating to sex education (where it is offered);
   - the hours spent on teaching during the normal school week, including religious education, but excluding the statutory daily act of collective worship, registration, and breaks (including lunch);
   - the dates of school terms and half-terms for the next school year;

[1] The regulations described in this section refer to LEA-maintained schools.

- a summary of each year group, indicating the content of the school curriculum and how it is organized, including in particular how National Curriculum subjects and religious education are organized, what other subjects and cross-curricular themes are included in the curriculum for all pupils, what optional subjects are available, and how choices among them are constrained;
- a list of the external qualifications (certificates) offered by examining bodies in specific subjects, approved under section 5 of the Education Reform Act, for which courses of study are provided for pupils of compulsory school age;
- the names of the syllabuses associated with the qualifications; a list of the external qualifications (certificates) offered by examining bodies in specific subjects, and the names of the associated syllabuses, offered to those beyond compulsory school age;
- details of any careers education provided, and the arrangements made for work experience;
- information about how to make a complaint, according to arrangements established under section 23 of the Education Reform Act;
- how to see and, where appropriate, acquire the documents to be made available under the regulations.

4. ask to see any schemes of work currently used by teachers in the school, or any syllabuses followed, whether for public examinations or otherwise.

These four sources of information must be made available to parents under the new regulations. In addition, any *entitled* person must have access to curricular records and any other educational records relating to a registered pupil and kept at the school. An entitled person is defined as a parent of a pupil under 16, both the parent and the pupil when the person is aged 16 or 17, and the pupil only when aged 18 or over. Access to the records must be provided within fifteen school days of the request being made, and there is a system for a written request for corrections if the records are considered to be inaccurate. Schools have had to keep these individual curricular records from September 1990. The records should indicate how each child is progressing in all areas of the National

Curriculum, including the levels reached in the profile components of each subject where these exist.

These developments were reinforced in October 1991 by the publication of the Parent's Charter. This reiterated some of the regulations already in force but it also added a full range of information to which parents could have access. The charter includes five documents which parents have a right to receive:

- an annual report on the child;
- regular reports from independent inspectors;
- performance tables for all local schools;
- a prospectus or brochure about the school;
- an annual governors' report on the school.

It also gives fuller specification to the form that the annual report to parents should take:

- comments on the pupil's progress in National Curriculum subjects;
- the pupil's level of attainment in each subject at the end of each key stage following statutory assessment at ages 7, 11, 14, and 16;
- results of other examinations or tests taken during the year;
- comments on the pupil's achievements in other subjects beside those of the National Curriculum and in other activities;
- comparison between the individual's results in examinations and national tests and those of others in the same group, and the national average;
- a comment from the headteacher or class teacher on general progress and attendance record;
- an indication of the person to whom the parent should talk to discuss the report, and details of how to fix an appointment.

So far the legal requirements have been described. Most, if not all, schools will be making arrangements that go beyond this. For example:

- There may be special parents' evenings when the curriculum for a particular subject or one year group is described in detail.
- Schools may provide visiting 'days' or 'times' when parents can drop in and observe classes. Timetable structures often make this easier at primary than secondary school, although at the secondary level parents' evenings may include 'sample' lessons with parents as pupils!

- The child's individual class teacher or tutor may make arrangements for contact at times when parents have particular concerns or queries.
- Annual reports to parents may be linked to an individual interview with the class teacher or tutor. At secondary level, subject specialists may also be available to help interpret the reports.

A good school welcomes parental interest and enquiries. It is, of course, important to remember just how busy a good school is. To turn up without warning and demand to see all the documentation described in this section would be unreasonable. It is also important to remember the importance of establishing the best possible relationship with schools and teachers. Some parents (and even some governors) have been known to approach the school with an element of suspicion, perhaps giving the impression of trying to catch someone out.

Through the 1990s all schools will be working out the most appropriate ways of developing the National Curriculum. Teachers are participating in training courses. Primary teachers have had to initiate a particularly wide range of new approaches. Allowance should be made for this in looking at a school's arrangements. On the other hand, parents should not be too meek in seeking out information or in ensuring that their child is receiving the full range of curriculum opportunities to which they are entitled. If anyone really feels that the school is not fulfilling the letter of the law, then section 23 of the Education Reform Act ensures that each LEA must establish arrangements for considering complaints from parents. Every school prospectus, as has been shown, must contain information about how a complaint can be made.

Beyond all this, parents are now encouraged to take an interest in their child's progress through the curriculum. If, from the earliest age, children are made to feel that the different school subjects and topics are of intrinsic interest, this will have great advantages for their later experience of schooling. Model-making kits, books, atlases, and colourful magazines all help with this. Some special National Curriculum books and materials have appeared on the market. It would be wrong to be critical of all these, but two things should be remembered:

- The National Curriculum is not an examination. Books that are really only an 'exam crib' should be avoided.

- The National Curriculum should not become burdensome to the child; this would be a severe blow to motivation and probably attainment. Any work at home should grow naturally from the school curriculum, and not be a means of forcing or pushing the child further than he or she need be at a particular stage.

Governors

Many of the concerns of parents and governors overlap. Governors have a particular responsibility to be responsive to the needs and interests of parents. They also have legal responsibilities for implementing the National Curriculum, and these must be clear to anyone taking the role of governor.

Every school has a governing body. The size varies with the size of the school, but it is usually made up of a combination of parents, teachers, LEA appointees, and co-opted governors. Headteachers have the choice of becoming governors, and the vast majority choose to join the governing board with full voting rights. All governors are appointed for a four-year term.

Under their curriculum responsibilities, governors must:

- ensure that the National Curriculum is implemented within the total school curriculum. They are also responsible for ensuring that provision of religious education meets the requirements of the law;
- prepare a school statement of policy, bearing in mind the LEA's curriculum statement policy and ensuring, of course, that all the requirements of the National Curriculum are met;
- determine the length of the school day and teaching sessions, within the data set by LEAs for terms and half-terms;
- receive complaints from parents about the way the National Curriculum is working. If governors fail to satisfy the parent then the LEA-agreed arrangements for complaints may be brought into operation;
- agree and determine school financial expenditure, much of which will be linked to the implementation of the National Curriculum;
- hold an annual meeting to which a written report of the work of the school and the activities of the governors must be presented—the report must be distributed at least two weeks prior

to the meeting. Examination, and where appropriate National Curriculum assessment, results must be included in the report;

- submit annually to the LEA information about the educational provision they are making for pupils including points where the National Curriculum has been modified for certain pupils;
- submit information about curriculum modifications for pupils who are the subject of a statement (see Chapter 7).

In schools that have opted for grant maintained status governors are not required to make the same links with LEAs that are set out above. In carrying out their duties, however, governors in all schools will work closely with the headteacher and other teachers. The statement of curriculum policy, for example, may be drawn up following discussion of a draft prepared by the headteacher and other members of staff and by reference to the curriculum policy of the local education authority. The annual return of information about the curriculum will almost certainly be drawn up by teaching staff. If a pupil, perhaps through illness or because of behaviour difficulties, has to have the National Curriculum modified for a period of time, the governors will be advised by the headteacher. Governors do have significant responsibilities for the curriculum, however, and they will need to become conversant with the terminology of the particular approach adopted by the school. Most schools now arrange for governors to spend time in classes. At secondary level, particular governors may take an interest in different parts of the curriculum, although they should also be aware of the strategies adopted for whole-curriculum planning. Governors have an important role to play in making sure that curriculum arrangements are described clearly to parents. Technical and obscure professional terminology should be avoided. To fulfil these responsibilities, governors need to have more than a cursory understanding of the issues involved.

9 Revising the National Curriculum

In 1993 a major review of the National Curriculum was carried out by Sir Ron Dearing, Chairman of the Schools Curriculum and Assessment Authority. The government accepted his recommendations in full and a revised National Curriculum will be introduced in time for the new school year beginning in September 1995. It is likely that the subjects will look very similar although the statements of attainment and attainment targets will be slimmed down. The language and terminology will remain unchanged, however, and although now only applicable to Key Stages 1–3, the ten levels scale has been retained. The review has introduced a number of modifications which are briefly summarized below:

- The statutory orders in all subjects will be reduced in order to free, in Key Stages 1–3, at least 20% of teaching time for use as the school thinks fit.
- The review will look at the curriculum as a whole for each key stage in producing recommendations for slimming down subject content. The statutory orders will be divided into core and optional elements.
- Schools are encouraged to use the time freed up to support work in the basics of literacy, oracy, and numeracy, as well as other subjects inside or outside the National Curriculum.
- Greater choice at Key Stage 4 allowing opportunities for vocational and broader academic options requires a reduction in the mandatory requirements. English, mathematics, single science, PE, and shorter courses in a modern foreign language and technology are retained as minimum requirements. RE and sex education must also be taught separately as though existing subjects, and careers education is noted as particularly important at this stage.

- The review sets as an objective the introduction of general national vocational qualifications (GNVQs) into Key Stage 4, although development work on how this is to be done has to be set in hand.
- When the newly revised curriculum is introduced in September 1995 it is proposed that there should be no further changes for at least five years.
- The ten-level scale as it existed in the first years of the National Curriculum was seen as 'increasingly complex and excessively prescriptive'. It does provide a useful means of monitoring progress and will, it is hoped, be more effective with a slimmed down curriculum. It is not aimed at Key Stages 1–3. At Key Stage 4 GCSE and the A–E grading system will be used to assess pupil performance.

Overall, in the terms set by the review, the revisions will seek to:

(i)   reduce the volume of material required by law to be taught
(ii)   simplify and clarify the programmes of study
(iii) reduce prescriptions so as to give more scope for teachers' professional judgement
(iv)   ensure the orders are written in an accessible way that maximizes the support given to the work of classroom teachers.

10 Controversial and Unresolved Issues

This guide seeks to describe and explain the National Curriculum. Inevitably, given the scope and scale of the changes, there are now many publications critical of the structure of the National Curriculum, the way it has been set up, and the approaches adopted in particular subject areas.

By 1993, for example, the concern of parents and teachers about the testing arrangements, the difficulties of implementing subjects such as technology, and the general worry about the curriculum as a whole being complex and over-prescribed led to the establishment of an actual review. This was led by Sir Ron Dearing, the first chairman of the Schools Curriculum and Assessment Authority. His findings, published in 1993, were accepted by the government and have been incorporated into this guide. Controversy, however, is likely to continue for some time and, as in any open democratic society, to be sustained as long as a central legislation exists. This section does not attempt to do justice to all the unresolved issues surrounding the National Curriculum; rather, ten issues that government, parents, and teachers may become involved with are listed, and the Further Reading section (below) provides the means for investigating each further.

Fitting everything in

One of the biggest difficulties of the National Curriculum was the overcrowding of the curriculum within subjects and across the curriculum as a whole. The interim Dearing review commented on this.

The National Curriculum is defined at present in a detailed and prescriptive way. This level of prescription stemmed no doubt from the belief that the National Curriculum, if it is to raise standards, should map the ground to be covered in an unambiguous way. But teachers have found that the degree of detail and prescription intrudes into the proper exercise of professional judgement, and tends to diminish the quality of the educational experience they can offer.

In primary schools, children should be allowed to pursue individual interests, follow up projects, and so on. This is equally true at secondary level, where it will be important to ensure a healthy take-up of a second foreign language and subjects such as drama and dance. The detailed and prescriptive way in which the National Curriculum was set out required so much attention that other things became neglected. This was particularly true at key stage 4, when a full programme of National Curriculum GCSE subjects left little room for studying any other subject.

The review of the National Curriculum is reducing the amount of time in subjects other than English, mathematics, and science that must be given to teaching the statutory, legally binding parts of the subject orders. There is also agreement that only the core foundation subjects should be compulsory in full at key stage 4 (technology and modern languages will be compulsory but can be studied as a short course).

There still remains a great deal of work at the national and school level to plan a whole curriculum at each of the four stages. This is likely to be one of the most important educational issues for debate and development in the middle years of the 1990s.

Subjects missed out of the National Curriculum

One of the criticisms of the National Curriculum is that the subjects are rather old-fashioned. Apart from technology, the list could have come out of a 1950s grammar school (or even one of the new secondary schools in the early 1900s). Although the National Curriculum does not have to be taught in subjects, it does have a strong influence on the way people think and the way the curriculum is planned. Many people point particularly to the way in which art and music are stipulated, as opposed to the more broadly based approach (adopted by most primary and an increasing number of secondary schools) of creative arts generally. In other words, are the arts going to become the low-status part of the National Curriculum? Home economics teachers are also concerned about the status and importance of their subject if it is subsumed within technology.

Debate about these issues is continuing today and may influence future revisions of the statutory orders. Perhaps one of the most pressing issues is how to ensure that the curriculum at key stage 4 provides opportunities for vocational and subject-based study. The 1988 plans gave little scope for this and issues noted by the Dearing review. The introduction of more flexible subject requirements at key stage 4 means that schools can now begin to plan a curriculum which takes account of vocational interests and allows some planning across the 14–18 or 19 age range rather than just to 16.

Planning across the curriculum

Many of the areas left out of the National Curriculum, for example environmental education, economic awareness, and citizenship, must now be taught with and across the programmes of study and attainment targets of the subjects. These topics involve highly significant issues for the last decade of the twentieth century. How are schools ensuring that they are covered? Are they really seen to be important by teachers, parents, and pupils?

Dated content

England and Wales now have some of the most detailed curriculum requirements in the world. Knowledge in many areas, particularly in science and technology, evolves rapidly. Taking another perspective, some people have argued that many parts of the statutory curriculum (for example in history) are culturally biased and need modification. Will it be possible to revise the statutory orders sufficiently quickly to keep them up to date and responsive to changing social attitudes and values?

Recording achievement

In Chapters 2 and 4 the question of achievement was discussed at some length. There is still a great way to go in providing assessment evidence that is reliable and fair and gives useful information to teachers, pupils, and parents, and that can be used in judging how well the school as a whole is doing. Some experts say that different forms of assessment should be used for different purposes. For example, one needs to assess in one way to give detailed information on how well an individual pupil is doing and in another way to measure how well a school, or all the pupils in a particular year, are progressing. Other people argue for a more informed approach. Much of the debate is technical, and in the early years the National Curriculum became embroiled in an over-simplistic and very political 'pro-testing/anti-testing' debate. The issue will not be resolved quickly or easily, although the Dearing review in 1993 recognized that the first attempt at assessment had been too time-consuming and too complex.

Giving parents information

As Chapter 8 described, parents now have the right to a range of information about the curriculum and their child's progress. This ought to be seen as a minimum requirement, and not as the full extent of the obligation. In good schools parents are given information about a wide variety of curriculum plans and activities. They are also shown how their help and encouragement can ensure that children progress with confidence and security.

Equal opportunities issues

There is now considerable evidence to show that certain groups of pupils are disadvantaged within the school curriculum. Research evidence suggests, for example, that girls are often disadvantaged by the design of tests and examinations. Children with certain special needs do not always receive the support they should. Ethnicity is also an issue in which inequalities have been extensively researched. Schools are expected to monitor the curriculum and assessment results, and try to remedy any difficulties that arise. How this is done, however, is controversial and open to a variety of different approaches.

Resources

Many teachers argue that insufficient attention has been paid to the resources needed for the National Curriculum. The statutory orders in some instances involve the wholesale revision of textbooks. Schools find it difficult to restock across a whole subject. There are also the costs of new equipment for subjects such as technology, and especially for information technology. The science programme involves primary schools in ongoing consumable supplies that were not previously required. Finally there is the issue of staff training, and whether the money conceded by the government is sufficient to meet these needs.

Teacher shortages and skills

Now that every school has to provide a National Curriculum, the problems of providing appropriately qualified teachers are clearly revealed. Finding sufficient numbers of science, technology, or modern language teachers is proving difficult in many parts of the country. There are shortages in other subjects such as mathematics and even English. In some years, particularly when the economy is growing, insufficient numbers of people come forward to train in these areas, and the difficulties therefore cannot be resolved quickly. There are also some shortages that are important, but less easy to observe. Some teachers of subjects such as English and mathematics have no qualification in the subject. It is important to ensure that they are receiving adequate additional training, support, and guidance. Similarly, in primary schools where teachers have to teach across the range of the National Curriculum, it is highly unlikely that any teacher will have sufficient grasp of all the subjects. Training and help are needed (and primary teachers rarely have the 'non-contact' time usually allocated to secondary-school teachers). It is a challenge to provide the necessary support without too much disruption to existing classes.

The time-scale for revision

In 1988 there was very little thought about how frequently the National Curriculum statutory requirements should be revised. Almost immediately two types of revision were proposed. The first was when the statutory requirements for a subject proved difficult to implement (technology, for example) or when the structure of the statutory orders proved cumbersome (the number of attainment targets in mathematics and science were reduced). The second was where political controversy surrounded the way the statutory orders were agreed (in English and history, for example, political interest groups, sometimes with the ear of government, have been arguing the pros and cons of traditionalist or more contemporary versions). The National Curriculum in principle is now generally accepted, and the Dearing review of 1993 has gone some way to resolving some of the more difficult issues. A five-year moratorium on change is proposed from September 1995. It remains to be seen, however, whether unpredictable political interventions will continue to present problems for teachers and schools, who need to be able to develop medium- and long-term plans.

Further Reading

Information about the National Curriculum can become dated very quickly. It is important, therefore, in looking for the statutory requirements, to purchase the relevant folders, such as *Science in the National Curriculum* or *Mathematics in the National Curriculum* (there is one for each of the subjects). They can be ordered through booksellers or direct from:

HMSO
P O Box 276
London SW8 5DT.

Each of the national councils also has an information section, producing a variety of helpful literature, including some specialist leaflets for parents and employers. The addresses are:

Schools Curriculum and Assessment Authority
Newcombe House
45 Notting Hill Gate
London W11 3JB.

SCAA Wales
Phase 2, East Buildings
Ty Glas Road
Llanishen
Cardiff CF4 5WE.

SCAA Northern Ireland
Rathgate House
Balloo Road
Bangor
County Down BT19 2PR.

Additionally, the Department for Education and Science, and the Welsh Office, publish regulations and advisory documents:

DFE
Sanctuary Buildings
Great Smith Street
Westminster
London SW1P 3BT.

DFE; Welsh Office
Crown Building
Cathays Park
Cardiff CF1 3NQ.

DFE; Northern Ireland (DENI)
Rathgate House
Balloo Road
Bangor
County Down BT19 2PR.

A number of books have now been published that describe the historical and political origins of the National Curriculum. Two authors—Denis Lawton and Clyde Chitty—have together and separately produced four interesting critical volumes:

Chitty, C. (1987), *Towards a New Education System: The Victory of the New Right?*, Falmer Press.

Lawton, D. (1989), *Education, Culture and the National Curriculum*, Hodder & Stoughton.

Lawton, D., and Chitty, C. (1988), *The National Curriculum*, Bedford Way Series, Institute of Education, University of London.

Lawton, D. (1992), *Education and Politics in the 1990s: Conflict or Consensus?* Falmer Press.

The most authoritative account of the whole of the 1988 Education Reform Act, including the curriculum clauses, is in Stuart Maclure's *Education Re-formed*, Hodder & Stoughton (1989).

The Open University is producing a number of courses focusing on National Curriculum issues. 'Curriculum and Learning', first presented in 1991, includes text, television films, audio-cassettes, and readers, and also includes a discussion of a number of aspects of the National Curriculum. One of the readers—Bob Moon (ed.), *New Curriculum: National Curriculum*, Hodder & Stoughton, 1991—includes a number of critical analyses of the period leading up to the implementation of the new legislation.

A journal, the *Curriculum Journal*, published three times a year by Routledge for the Curriculum Association, is a valuable source of comment and analysis.

Schools and local authority advisory services will also be able to provide advice on publications which report the latest legislative developments in the National Curriculum.

List of Abbreviations

AoE	Area of Experience
APU	Assessment of Performance Unit
AT	Attainment Target
CAI	Common Assessment Instrument
CCW	Curriculum Council for Wales
CFS	Core Foundation Subject
DES	Department of Education and Science
DfE	Department for Education
FS	Foundation Subject
HMI	Her Majesty's Inspectorate
HSU	Historical Study Unit
IT	Information Technology
KAL	Knowledge about Language
LEA	Local Education Authority
LoA	Level of Attainment
MFL	Modern Foreign Languages
NC	National Curriculum
NCC	National Curriculum Council
NISEAC	Northern Ireland Schools Examination and Assessment Council
PoS	Programme of Study
SAT	Standard Assessment Target
SCAA	Schools Curriculum and Assessment Authority
SDU	School-designed Unit
SEAC	Schools Examination and Assessment Council
SoA	Statement of Attainment
SO	Statutory Orders
TGAT	Task Group on Assessment and Testing

Sources and Acknowledgements

pp. 5, 12, 51   NCC (1992) *Starting out with the National Curriculum*, York

pp. 18–19   Average Mathematics Proficiency and Average Science Proficiency graphs, from 1989 Report by the Center for the Assessment of Educational Progress in the U.S.A.

p. 26   Webb, R., (1993) *Eating the Elephant Bit by Bit: The National Curriculum at KS2*, published by Association of Teachers and Lecturers (ATL) London

p. 33   Extracts from *A Guide to Teacher Assessment*, published by the Secondary Examinations and Assessment Council (SEAC)

pp. 33–5   Dearing, R., (1993) *The National Curriculum and its Assessment: An interim report*. NCC and SEAC

pp. 42–5   Cox, C. B., (1991) *Cox on Cox: An English Curriculum for the 90s*, Hodder and Stoughton

pp. 42–45   DES, (1989) *Report of the English Working Party 5–16* (The Cox Report), HMSO, London

p. 53   DES, (1988) *Report of the Committee of Inquiry into the Teaching of the English Language* (The Kingman Report) HMSO London

pp. 55–7   SCAA (1994) Examples of test questions from Key Stage 3 English Tier 4–7 Sample Papers 1 and 2, and Key Stage 1 Assessment Handbook (English)

p. 56   NICC, (1990), *Guidance Materials for English*

p. 59   DES/WO (1988) *Mathematics for Ages 5–16: Proposals of the Secretary of State for Education and Science, and Secretary of State for Wales*, HMSO London

pp. 60–1   NCC (1991), *Mathematics: Non-statutory guidance*, York

pp. 63–5   SCAA (1994) Examples of test questions from Key Stage 3 Mathematics Tier 6–8 Sample Paper 1, and Key Stage 1 Pupil and Source Sheet Booklet

pp. 78–80   SCAA (1994) Examples of test questions from Key Stage 3 Science Tier 5–7 Specimen Paper 1, and Science Key Stage 1 Pupil Sheet Booklet

pp. 109–10   NICC (1991) *Guidance Materials for History*

pp. 110–12   CCW, (1991), *Non-Statutory Guidance for History*

pp. 112–14   DES, (1991) *History in the National Curriculum*

pp. 120–3   DES/WO, (1991) *MFL in the National Curriculum*

pp. 124–5   DES/WO, (1990) *MFL for ages 5–16*

pp. 126–31   DES/WO, (1991) *Art for Ages 5–16*

pp. 134–7   DES, (1992) *Music in the National Curriculum (England)*, HMSO

pp. 138–41   DES, (1992) *Physical Education in the National Curriculum*, HMSO